D1557238

6

PASSAGE
Selected Poems
1943–1978

PASSAGE

Selected Poems

1943–1978

Louis Coxe

University of Missouri Press
Columbia & London, 1979

Copyright © 1979 by
The Curators of the University of Missouri
Library of Congress Catalog Card Number 78–20382
Printed and bound in the United States of America
University of Missouri Press, Columbia, Missouri 65211
All rights reserved

Library of Congress Cataloging in Publication Data

Coxe, Louis Osborne, 1918–
    Passage: selected poems, 1943–1978.

    I. Title.
PS3505.O9367P55   811'.5'2   78–20382
ISBN 0–8262–0260–8

"Marsh Hawk" and "Hannah Dustin" first appeared
    in the *Hudson Review.*
"Squaring the Circle," "Time Out," "The Lake,"
        "The Offering," "From the Window Down,"
        "Hero's Winter," and "Bringing in the Float"
        first appeared in the *New Yorker.*
"Union Soldier" first appeared in *Furioso.*
"Swift's Tomb in St. Patrick's" first appeared in *Poetry.*
"Barred Owl" first appeared in *Transatlantic Review.*
"Idyl" first appeared in *Dubliner.*
"E. A. Robinson: Head Tide" and "Keys"
        first appeared in *University.*
"Spring Near the Airbase" first appeared in the *Nation.*
"The Passage" first appeared in *The Second Man*
        © 1955 by the University of Minnesota Press.
"The Middle Passage" first appeared in *The Middle Passage*
        © 1960 by the University of Chicago Press.

This book is published with the assistance of an
award from the American Council of Learned Societies.

Contents

PASSAGE

Selected Poems
1943–1978

The Offering

Summer turns in sleep: trumpet-vine
Bells of nasturtium and campanula blown
And blare midafternoon that day I am nine
And alone in a wide space of time light and sea:
I knew I was at home
And where I went, me.

How it all comes back, wind in the telephone wires and grasses,
Over the sand-and-spray-blow, salt hay.
The north range travels in cloud-shadow passes
And I walk on water naked spirit
As closed a self and single as that day
None else shall inherit,

A gift to break hearts left me to save:
I inherit myself alive in air
In a form of sun, water, and wind that moves
Between two elements of near and far:
All that spirit loves flesh will require
And comes from somewhere toward me there
Not caring what it gives.

Timing

The brick cities of my childhood bloom
A rose light falling dark in rain:
Where the north river drained a rotten wound
Black mills rankled and ran down.

Over the stink of tanneries hung still at noon
Coal plunged metal chutes to cellar bins:
I shudder back on the shock wave of sounds
Reeking brightness against the dark of home.

Black winter roads, spring gutters on the run,
East wind shifting summer, chestnut falls:
I have gone a longer way than light-year miles
Or earth's progress round the sun.

The Passage

The rain blows silver from blue sky
Aslant upon my vessel's steel:
Maui to starboard, Molokai
To port. Between, the world I wheel.

The squall blows back and walks the wake
And sun draws steam from metal, blue
With wet while Maui quivers like
A lover waiting to come true.

Between these islands heart is fed:
Between two waters, salt and fresh
The spirit drinks a life it bled
And sun moves kindly on the flesh.

Let Maui far to starboard shift
Her shoulder, let the rainsquall blow
On Molokai, on lava-drift
And lepers whiter there than snow.

The Lake

The light that labored to an early fall
Fell in the woods like rain secret and spare
And where the autumn road ran to a sprawl
At the lake's edge four geese blundered into air
And seemed to pluck my breath in foil of wings
That scooped the gathering dark and in their ache
For height to take a rhythm from those springs
The heart feeds for the feeding of a lake—

That lake where autumn calls in brant and blue,
The whistling swan, all game and under gun,
Doomed and in wild beauty dear those few
In pride that preen before the death of sun.
Upward with unseen purchase still they foil
The fallen heart with height as still they quest
For other feeding, one dark more to coil
Around them perfect still until the last.

Spring Near the Airbase

A jet from the airbase wailing out of sight
Cuts in her afterburner rolling time
And space out flat and level with her height
While under the trailing sound geese start their climb
Heavy, unheard, and straggling toward their aim
As though this spring had summoned each by name.

The radar search planes bound for Newfoundland
Go over the fisherman's drag or mackerel seine:
Whether at ebb or flood, the tide shall stand
Eternal to their height, the coast of Maine
Curve out its coves, vectors of course and speed,
Pips on a scope, a fallen magnitude.

Unclouded quadrants gather to a sphere:
Weather from here to Gander rare as glass
Tiers in a choir of engines hunting air
And radar flinching at the touch of mass.
High beyond birds and rigid under noon,
The planes seek home unpeopled as the moon.

Haying

I tramp on hay two oxen draw:
The ricks of summer slanting sway
On a sea-sloping field and flaw
Bursts sunstarts on Saint Mary's Bay.

Treading in timothy waist-high
I pile the salt air up with scents
Grassy and hot—gratuity
For man and his yoked ruminants.

Beyond the seawall where the weir
Stakes all on tide, Saint Mary sends
One tramp hull down, her stack a smear,
And three terns shifting as their winds

And I grown up in mows of grass
Hold up to heaven and salt air
A grace the heart will shrink to guess
When time has yoked it to despair.

Red Right Returning

This red nun on my left hand leans away
From land's last fingerings and with the tide
Strains gauntly for the hundred-fathom curve:
From here on, navigator, let the sea decide.

Behind lie promises that in our wash
Leap to fulfillment like this fairway nun
And both are naked in dependency,
Trusting horizon when the ship has gone.

And this was known before: I come from coasts
Whose days are seaward looking, where the hills
Grew round with watching for the China barks
And mackerel seiners hustling to their sails.

And I have need of all sea-silent men
Whose prophecy found witness in their sons:
Very and Hawthorne held their loneliness
By right of heritage and trampling winds.

Be with me now, you travelers into hearts,
And bring me lucky through each threatened night
That I may keep my promises and find
Known channels with a red nun on my right.

Marsh Hawk

Before dew falls and dark has clutched horizon
He comes, tilting with shadow, from his marsh
Cruising the meadow, stooping and all vision
For white-footed mice ascuttle under slash.

Late vetch, Queen Anne's lace, soiled yarrow
Stand still under that lambency of flight
As his brownness darkens against bay and alder—
Death in the vein of evening bringing night.

Curved now like space as the cove curves to the water
His talons creep with hunger while the cruel
Mandibles shudder to the ghost of savor
And the eyes throw light as frozen as a jewel.

He homes in on the fear that sweats the weather
A bearing perfect in a strike of blood
Gripping within its purchase night and hunger,
The cast of shade, the certain ebb and flood.

Et in Acadia

Champlain to the Sagamore Membertou

Membertou my late friend, I write these lines
For both of us, and if only I could post them when I'm done
Over your grave among our favorite pines
Bordering my arbor (built to remind me of home),
Wherever you are you would read them, as in times
Long gone in Acadia you first read Champlain.

What a grasping ignorant wild lot we were,
Not sense enough to work out with the cold
Where life lives—hard, yes, but striking fire
As you rub against your world. No, we had to build
Each his own disease, ache and despair
And heat up quarrels out of the hate we held.

How I almost broke my heart for a westward passage
And told you—you, chuckling and at ease in smoke
Marvelling the oversea itch crawling this white personage
As though desires and pox made the one crude joke.
Your body upright underground with its simple appanage
Mocks, as you never did, with dissolution what I spoke.

Such heartbreak country yours, those rare gardens, field
            forest and stream:
You and your people haunt me old friend and I yearn
For the north hills purple at evening—the last end of my dream
There it was, true among you all, but I must burn
For west, for moving, and in going from home
I killed you with my sickness being white mad and an alien born.

Idyl

Lovers who meet each other
Under cover of dark
Grind a single hunger
Against a thirst to spark
A heat for the brain's fever
Or the craze of a heart.

The owl wild in the wood
The blind mole under ground
Shall meet at dusk in blood
And single of hunger find
An end not understood.

From the Window Down

I follow from my window down
The paths my children's feet have mown
Running to the rim of bank
Where I stood once. Yarrow is rank,
Saint Johnswort straggles at the verge,
The paths like past and future merge
In a single child, myself or mine,
Poised there a season out of time,
And blown like the burrowing swallow he
Shall next in time drop down to sea
Dropping below my sight to find
Salt desolation: I am blind:
Another watched me so. I gaze
And see myself, a child, and raise
The head that I held so before
The bank undid me to the shore.

Hero's Winter

Leaf by leaf the days descend
And let the light in and the cold:
By night the widening windows fend
More black away. By morning gold
Drips softly to ground:
Oakleaf, laurel are mold.

It seems an opening out, a spell
Of vistas binding head to heart.
The eye sinks higher in a well
Of blue, now leaves have blown apart
And winds whirl with a will
In the naked yard.

Snow comes out of this, I know:
Out of the open sky comes in
Deciduous heaven. It shall throw
Deceit in white across the lawn
Eager at sills and slow
But sure to win.

Let strip heart and house and trees—
Weather shall never find me wide.
My doors are double. Let it freeze!
I keep the fallen year inside
Green forever with deeds
And blown with pride.

Lady of The Freesias

Deep stars—blue yellow white and red
Streaked with tender glanular secret veinings
Each trembling on a bare green stem
They baffle against the winter windows
And daze the whole room with scent.

Upward to light only to fall dark
After a senseless bloom. It was your hand
And desire that woke them, spoke
Touched and felt them to that end
As to make life with beauty, given luck.

Queen over tender blossoms as they burn,
You watch them fade and quench, all failing stars,
Sending them back to dark, since what they were
May, given luck, return,
Granted such gift as yours.

Swift's Tomb in Saint Patrick's

Stripped to his legend like an Irish war
the madman lies under a name in bronze.
Above him tramp the heels of girls and deans
statesmen and tourists come on business here.
How can the heart find grace or peace before
its God, knowing that fury in the stones?
Can Stella pray now? whose unshielded glance
stoned her forever in a trodden floor?
High in the choir cry the English dead:
the few loved far away in England call:
outside, the Romans, broken up like bread
move to their marvels, know him not at all
who studied hate lest pity turn him mad
and wore love's seamless fabric like a pall.

E. A. Robinson: Head Tide

The road's hard black now, but the pheasant colors
Of fall, the dwindling Sheepscot, the meetinghouse hill
And the houses have not changed in the hundred years
Since the brave season painted for your first fall.

No soul stirs, no wind, the river barely runs
But I feel you pass on your river walk and hear
Bare feet in the dust and smell the Gravensteins
You ruminate while an old man bends your ear.

I see what you saw: the hero turns to child,
Jack to giant, both gone uphill into sky
Where pine and hardwoods clash, mingle and fold,
You and he black there—fierce on the eye
As the fire of this fall day flares in cold.

Hannah Dustin

(the statue in Pennacook)

The red veins in the Gravensteins
Started before the frost. I felt
Desire move my blood where vines
And trees hid fruit I only smelt.
That day when windfalls cost me dear
The Indian burning in his stain
Caught up my solitude. His fire
Ran on my house eaves dense as rain.

Across the brush he dragged my hate
The miles of Merrimac to north
Where captives stied like pigs were bait
To tempt our kin and vengeance forth.
I would not weep though he splashed out
My child's brains on a beech's root:
God mocks the mockers: with each gout
Bright on the bark I tasted fruit,
And let the red man drink his night
Myself unfearing. Fear had laced
His liquor had he known how tight
I filled with poison for his taste.
Drunken he pressed me where he heaped
The bed of boughs. When lust griped hard
I felt his knife, unmanned him, reaped
And sickled through his groin like lard.
His heart leaped once, I struck him there,
Blood ran like fire on my breast.
I walked and felt the dark for hair
Sliming my hands. I scalped the rest

And lashing the lids about my thighs
Fled naked to the boat alone.
The years have run me down. I rise
In fire frozen to a stone.

Nelson's Pillar

The crest that tossed him there
Topgallant in his place
Ebbs fast and far.
Traffic snarls at his base
Though the tall head lifts clear

Over all battles he goes,
Sail, turbine, oar.
He has claimed honor in rogues,
Fidelity in a whore:
Passion is what he knows.

Metal and men leave a trail
Betraying the course they run.
Aloft, the admiral
Steers for the sound of the guns
And crowds-on sail.

And still red on horizon
The fires he woke and fed
Burst on the sight with vision
Raising the long dead
Who brought their flesh to his passion
And blood down on his head.

Union Soldier

South and west from the tiding of Calais Maine
In the tousled commons squared off by elms
He grows in local stone grey on the green
Like a hull a bight becalms
And stock-still on the granite plinth can see
Under the kepi through the blind stone eyes
His land slipping from him between
Towns leveling to prairie and the terrible skies
Of rotting Hollywood and Los Angeles.

Whoever botched him into statue knew
Skill out of place for this, grace out of order.
The grounded gun no more familiar grew
Or shapelier to him, murder
Less than his rebel blood running him aghast
From Bull Run and the squealing enemy behind.
And died in the shallows, tramped askew
Under the hot passage of the southern wind
To rot for richer texture in that ground.

Now he is stone. Topsfield, Litchfield, towns
Moving to bloody Kansas tore their quarries
To tier him up, blind anonym, for clowns
Touring the summer boroughs
And for the sliding vista of his land
Dropping beyond to newer monuments.
The eyes surpass three cairns
Of cannonballs, two fifteen-pounder guns,
The fieldpieces he learned and lived by once.

Quivering like the tune the tree toad yells
Here by last summer light, your heart
Can never hark back feeling the lumped hills
As he did burst apart
With shaken host of enemy horse and man
Crying on faith in what they killed for, lust

To hold on, violent cells
Calm at the center of their holy trust.
His land was north and winter to the touch.

And died in that country, part of the one land
Sloping from Saint Croix, died against his will,
Misled, the fool of folly, killed to stand
Today inland from ocean swell.
Erect, unreconciled, he moves against
The fumbling dark of trees, lighter than air,
Than your vision wiser. His hand
Along his left thigh empty as his stare
Waits for a sign, the ultimate cease-fire.

Mocker of all who will against heart's truth,
Soldier stand up, stone gunbutt at your heel:
The special man kills with the skill of youth,
Feels what two metals feel
Joined in the senseless torsion of a lathe
That holds him still against a working part
Bright to the eye. In death
He turns to slag. You in your blacked-out park
Bend the night back around you in an arc.

Third Person

I have to find my glasses first, then see
if I want to see. There's a blind way
between stone and staring, a misty
unedged distance. I think I know why:

What God fingered first was perfect, a man grown
between black and light. A woman—stranger
than self—keeps working a way back home
to grow to her own inside him like a cancer.

How feel a way out from that ribless cage?
Half blind, did I make shape of what I knew
and take it to heart, girl of that stone age
when I looked in glass and dark was what came through?

Barred Owl

The owl that hunted under autumn woods
Came to the oak where my window holds it in
To perch there staring, saintlike hollow-eyed,
Part of the bark and joining of a limb.

Below him mouse and mole froze into leaves
Pied dun and umber piling round the bole.
Heaven stayed still and earth. A window gives
On more than these: under them all is hell.

Was it from that gate that a black draft of three crows
Blew in a cry to hunt him from his wood?
A moment hung and steady in the glaze,
They left a hollow where a saint had stood.

Songbird

The vireo in the elm warbles all summer
Invisible and high in a bubble of song
A liquid boredom and longing without humor
Like the summer disquiets and transports of the young.

Unable to help itself and throat wide open,
Whatever's supposed to flow flows to its end:
Pure behavior, vireo by pattern,
He chortles his sole abstraction of a sound.

There are other and odder birds at lower stages
Who buzz, titter and shriek to speak their piece:
None of it means a thing except that the wages
Of song is death and singing has no price.

Time Out

As first light quivered in a sweat of ice
Crinkling ground zero, I saw time take flight:
I watched it rounding on a target space
While dawn broke on my left, moon bent on my right.

Shaped like a fountain before it doubles down
It steadied between two lights, broke from its path
As the moon ran under and sun climbed flights of clouds
To stand at a measureless angle out of breath.

I watched the archer reach back to his quiver
And notch an arrow—the string flung it aloft
Steady this time on the target's round forever
As though the prize rode easy on that shaft.

Keys

Sly as a miser, this key locks
Doom in my safe-deposit box:
Expired policies, a dud will,
Cards to credit me in hell.

Unanswerable mail and papers
Unplowed drift up my office tables:
That roundhead fretted like a saw
Must keep them till my conscience thaw.

As like that as a feckless twin
A third unlocks a door named "Men":
Beyond it, wastage waterborne
Roars to the winding of a horn.

This unlocks the door I shut
On the narrow house where I grew up,
Where I and the future fell estranged
Hiding behind locks we changed.

New Year's Eve

The tractor-trailer that hit slick ice and blew
its air brakes, jackknifed, broke apart and burst
halfway over the snow ridge parting Route
Ninety-five and trashed the traffic past
the tollbooth. The air resonated horn
hooter, siren striking the iron sky
to break a snowfall down that seemed to burn
in the red lamps, the flare-pots, the fire
of the wrecked cab. Up the northbound flue
traffic wisped easy like the rising wind
shuddering away from the cruisers' pulse-beat blue
each car listening for its stroke to end,
begin again, steady, chime like a peal
ringing a new world in, like something real.

God's Country

Two diesel rigs haul out past and slash
Rainwater too dense for the wiper-blade
And for a flash all of my world turns blind
At seventy plunging up the Jersey marsh;
Then it clears, again my world's six lanes of cars
Between the cracker-towers tipped with flares
And the tankers pumping crude straight from the heart.
A jet howls at Newark coming up for air.

Manhattan rears, there goes my garden state
Where the rain darkens long before the ground.
West of here's all heart, all south bleeds white,
Eastward runs asphalt to Long Island Sound
And I'm north for the sulphur rivers, the wrecker towns
Where the natives burn in their shacks for heat and light.

Morning Watch

That made a hard day's dying
out under the guns, labor
of seas doing, undoing
outside help or harbor.

This same self young that ages
now and faster moves back
through emblems of seeing, images
in water, wreck

and whatever spirit pondered
watch over watch breaks down
to the dream mishandled
and the thing undone

Old Dead People

(Provence)

By the wall the Romans broke
That old crowd died
All of them. It was their own dead
They worshiped and carved in stone
Each stone man with a right hand on his head—
Blessing? a holding down? The Roman plough
Went through and over and they rutted the plain:
Only ditches and rubble walls now
Cobble the sentinel hill
Where they built for safety, looking down.

The Romans spread like oil: from port to citadel
Their roads still run straight, rectify the land
They ploughed over and under ruin.
Legionary, centurion—tough and traveling light
With heavy weapons—broke till they were broken
And tractors turn the ground over their heads:
Where their roads met noons blaze
Under height so blue no cloud comes down
Laying on hands, or water saying grace.

Anniversary

This simple day breaks
Like water, like glass:
A splatter a soft crash
And our world's awake.

Am I alone here
Where the light travels
In squalls and fevers
Over the quivering air?

We are all losers
Water air and I
Helpless below a sky,
On a ground, of poisons.

Once love knew enough
Counting up to two
Now what I owe you,
You me, is cut in half.

Years sift and strain
Leave us our only lives
Castaways on our selves
We search for each other again.

Close in simple dark
One and one make two:
Taking the long way through
We make a marvel work.

Squaring the Circle

A bear cub chained and tethered to a stake
Prowled in a Humble service station yard
In a rubble of popcorn, apple cores, dumped cars
And tourists giving him 7-Up to drink.
He swept a centrifuge arc over arc
Like a windshield wiper, and his chain and collar clanked:
Four paces left—does freedom die that hard?—
Four paces right, till the center wound him back.
Beyond the dump, meadow and swamp meet trees
Grown dark as they crawl the Appalachian chain;
Ahead, the freeway flumes the traffic east,
Scatters sunlight and dips to the Gulf of Maine
Where the lobsterman prowls the hundred-fathom curve
And the yacht swings on her mooring like a slave.

Bringing in the Float

It looks like the old painterly palette
out here—my neighbor's son
reining the white float in, green dock
against blue water, two men
crouched over a come-along, hauling

while the river squalls and shrinks
in wrinkles, yellow and red
leaves stipple the eddy and follow
around a spiral of spring tide

and I feel my back creak but no strain.
It's a great Sunday morning to bring home
all the summer landings, to break clean
with a season, taking what will come.

33

Briar Island

Wait by the blue rocks over the jump of spray
Where we came from, gone back down
White under and over blue, day
Over and under in the fall wind blown
Not wondering why

You and I stand together where an island enters
The sea and the tide gathers against itself:
The ancients would see monster beasts; disasters
Unshapely we may see, silent ourselves with vision
Alone together with this island.

All the children all gone. We are raised high,
The wind presses against rock and surges the cliff grasses,
Lifts your hair. Your head I know. Here am I
With you—most of the time. And time presses
Hard, wind and tide turning the brute season.

Four Songs from Five Plays

1.

Never known before
this rock and river, sun
so low alongshore,
never seen noon
at solstice stand so still
and close in the wry grass.
Time to say grace
in hope, with thanks for fire
making a way north,
saying prayers for a birth.

Tides go up and down
in a river around the world.
Everything moves around
or burns. I've heard
of flight so far and pure
it came back standing out
unknowing, but sure
that going was its route
to the near by far.

2.

Back inside the cave again
out of the new cold. The walls
hang out old commercials, shapes of men
and angels, what we were then.
Some of us remember great vibes and sounds,
heat, trails in the sky. I know
only my mother cave where the old scribes
graphed the great market over stone.

Like war, waiting. Spasm. Plunge
coming home and trying to pass:
it's a change to run from, myself
gone swingeing back to grass.
Shield me now, set me down
an infant out of inner air
on edge at ocean, shell of sound
and echoing ear.

3.

Daytime nighttime love a little
rest. Does that tell it all?
Wait till after dark, the lift-off thrust
after the fall—
no, better to forget and go
out where the burning god moonwalking Apollo
strikes his precession west
and the Dipper bears north, cold heart
cold harbor picking out the pole.
Make a new start. The neighbor lights
go black, no wave
breaks in the eye. Turn back home, if you have
a home to keep and luck to heat it by
under the mariner stars where nothing lives.

4.

Lovers falling out of love
break apart, go
to any other, take leave
of sense. Love is what they know.

Hand and eye and body quiver
still to an old touch. New
signs across old senses cover
what they called a heart ago.

Love comes up, lies down, goes blind
inside another. Thinking one
and one make one at a time
no one can win—

not those games of kill and cure,
fear of falling, the rogue wave:
may these lovers learn care
before they earn their leave.

Möbius

Hear it out there winding the endless band
unbounded around whatever keeps the peace.
Is it sound that moves it crying toward an end
wound up from the beginning in its voice?

Remember those laser pulses, how they gathered
out in a field to an arc, a leap through space:
once one of us saw something turning a wild weather
seamless, untiring, creatures we suppose.
That was in the beginning, after the end
began again, turning up the gain:
no one walks there now around that bend
where finders might be keepers, going gone

On the Border

      (Saint Croix Country)

County by county it's a country fair
land-cruising, riding an easting down
over the blueberry barrens, fields of fire
growing green out of black address unknown

We know where we're going rimming the land
still fought for over frequencies so low
or high air only or angels learned the law
we take unknowing into our own hands

And the time changes, takes a departure west
into other quadrants where the hunter ghosts
travel the painted woods making up fires.
We go east, back of the known past
that comes round again making the country fair

Helix

Out there something bright is turning the snow
to a slow wraith, a devil
of snow-dust that drives
over the level field
into woods run wild.

Who's that turning white
set against the west?
Only the season ghost
or even less, light
frozen or almost.

Marvels have come and gone
prints on a palpable air,
whispers echoing escape
outside breathing together.
Listen: they key a pulse
over out there
escaping one another
close to something else.

Loyalist Graveyard, Acadia

Where we begin they ended, under ground
and far from home, beginning over again forever.
We have searched their titles looking to find
ourselves in other wars. We could take cover
here in Acadian country still falling apart
after empire. We might go home
to king country and western and not get hurt.
We'd do no harm.

Bring back Champlain alive here, or surprise
the shade of the old sachem Membertou in passage
over these stones? Nothing moves or grows
here but the rags of weed. Hope might forage
an instant here as it falters, folds—still part
of where it came from—despair
that ventures hope, wrong from the start:
a sick elm and a willow: dead air.

At Louisburg tories and wetbacks spend French leave
around the ruins. A middle-and-far east
lies here at the edge of ocean where the broken wave
of empire let them down. That was a ghost
who came to them by daylight crying Peace
in the Father's bosom and they followed Him
to this graveyard by the sea where fog and water pace
the seasons, time's old tourists, heading home.

Skywriting

Look out there where the window ends
in blinds and shades: the shadow runs
away to woods growing awry
in run-out pasture. Why not pry
the overhead that clamps a lid
on zero ground, the outer edge
of upward where there might be open
space to load with common human.

This may be the day: can you tell time
just checking pressures, your upper arm?
Flights of angels, codes, mixed bags
all taking to strangers. Will they take back?

Change curves inward, time implodes
to denser silences gone cold
here in the heart that fibrillates and chatters
alone, not caring, used to it, mutters
into the voice-tube its vital signs.
The weather promises. Everything ends,

but not out there: look through the pane
projecting billions, figures far
and away but always heading home.
Where is it? When? What's it for—
not what it is or can be, ever:
it's an end, a window, even a heaven
open to enter, to say grace
to the lucky who land there and know their place.

Triage

It's a wicked world they used to say—
say it again and let it ring!
Only the world inside can play
that game. It plays anything.

Which of the deadly seven kills
leaving no traces, nothing behind?
A lifelong study to get even
fills up the will, fixes the mind.

Shelter the seasons, sing to the branches,
follow water where it runs:
hate takes muscle, counts by ounces
and nobody loses who wins once.

Losses made up keep bodies counted:
triage, mercy, name your game.
Silence turns silver, a dream of islands
made out of mountains, a name for home.

The Devil You Know

Believing nothing, I still saw the king
of less than nothing painted like famine war
and wearing winter. He stank of fire
watering out. I think
he had heard me coming.

Along the turned flank of the black fell
a field tilts, meets rock and falls
to tide. I saw him there
where everything rises, turns in swirls
into middle air.

He had come to my calling, just where wrack and tide
met at the cleft of cliff, the sea threw
away a runnel staggering, gone white
as winter, wasting to lighter blue:
Keep to the devil you knew.

Will he go out with the tide changing the season?
I brought him there cold against western flame,
called him by my name. My name is Legion
and we are many. When I call, we come.

"As the sun sinks"

As the sun sinks deeper into a northern west
afternoon ages before its time:
Here it's the river crinkles, not concrete
or new late-comers who think east
nothing but light. Sun comes to a term
up against horizon, out late.

Why live here at all in this shrinking prison?
Nobody shut us in, it was our choice.
Against a coiling sky faked-out in lights
the winter ponders us. Has it a reason,
even a voice? not yet. It waits
forever and now, keeping its own season.

How life is small and the great matter little
up against the dark, the cold at heart
clenched around zero and the Big Bear settled
up against Polaris. Ringing around the meadow
the oaks brace up and hold the circle down
where it belongs. The sky keeps nothing on.

Where is it we live now beside winter weather
blacker by night picked out in stars
like Babylon? The skyscape stares
in a quiver, ice booms. Do you wonder whether
again time will come around, the first
making the last, beginning again all over?

Over the inlet, ice, and we skate our season
into the marsh, pine-and-hemlock friezed.
Evening begins in a levelling of horizon
our sun goes skidding around. The skates graze
against a blackness in passing, we meet the level line
of night still one another, never all alone.

We have all seen spirits walking water, ice
or air, even—a temper of wind that races
across a fall field, or the hush of a moon
between bald trees. Let us stay in place
till it comes again in a pillar of snow blown
over and closing highways, and as it rises
over us changing color and kind, comes down.

Chantey

The last great fortunes have been grown and felled:
tycoons, robber barons fell away like stones
out of the walls they built. Now the great cold
settles over Africa, seas rise
and everything will go under or freeze, the oil all sold.

Once the Nazi boats lit up our coast
torching tankers, bombers ran Europe down
in firestorm, Tokyo burst like a sun,
Churchill gave up Coventry to keep a code.

Those were the days. Nights? they ran red and black
as the world rolled over in sleep. Out on the Horn
of Africa now, down toward the Cape
the rebel right shifts left. Here, we're born
again and again, hoping against hope
someone will change our luck.

One more day my Johnny till we turn
her heading homeward on a quartering breeze.
Out of the west the east comes up. It will burn
and quench again, the missiles fire and freeze
coming and going, the first new fortune born
something out of nothing, a first prize.

Beginning Again

A son's child opening into light on water
and the self in shade under bright morning:
watch by the cliff edge, on a flower field
an unfolding steady as tide turning.

Nowhere runs wild in a moment of field flowers
and glacial rock. A child naked in light
stands up holding clover, grass wavers
around him, a stunning of sun in a white acre

where nothing moves but the heart that would call Time
knowing no better, maybe too late to learn.
The child stands there at land's end: the stand of tide
holding him up, and the flower, till the turn

The Middle Passage

The Middle Passage

I.

It was New England April at the docks:
You know the kind: wet wind, a threat of snow
While sky plays open and shut. That kind of day—
A fine day for hauling south by east
And making good your seven or eight knots.
The tide was full at seven, and by eight
Two Indiamen of Derby's with their sails
Loose at the bunts were ready for the wind,
And old man Derby stood on his own wharf
With his words of Godspeed and bring back the goods.
Across the slip, warped in at Crowninshield's,
The HAPPY DELIVERY, whaler, Captain Ames
Of Newport, waited for her supercargo.
Burns, the mate, had seen the orlop stowed
With water casks, the forepeak with supplies—
Horsebeans, salt beef and the captain's liquors.
The customs papers cleared and all hands waited
To sway up, set taut, let her take the wind,
But still no supercargo. Ames was below
With the owners—you remember Bliss and Crane?
I thought so! Well, they made their pile, perhaps
In ways that you and I—well, who's to say so?
Money makes money and you have to love it
And know your love is pure because it's yours.
Canot came on the pier then—you knew Canot
And you can see—the wagon beating the cobbles
Like a carronade. That brought the skipper up
Topside, the owners too. Canot jumped down.

This was his first voyage, mind you. Down he jumps
And "Morning, Captain Ames" he says. Old Ames
Lit up like a rum-blossom. "Mister Canot"—
The boy had run around to the pierhead caplog
And didn't answer. Back he comes with the men

Who were standing by the vessel's lines. "No fear.
I'll be aboard," he says and sets the men
To hauling out his gear and stowing it
Aboard the vessel. "Mind the chest," says Canot
Leaning against the tailgate with his eye
Cocked to the quarterdeck. "Those are medicines
In case you lads get clap somewhere down south. . ."
"You get us ashore and we'll get us the clap,"
One of them growls and hefts the medicine chest
And Canot laughs—you know that laugh of his—
While Ames turns a redder shade. "Mister Canot . . ."
But Bliss had plucked his arm and walked him off,
His thin beard wagging—you can see the style
And guess the words. Yes, Bliss had hired Canot:
Bliss knew his man—knew men too well, I think,
While Crane kept books and pared the rinds and wages.
A handsome couple! You might have seen Bliss say
"Let him alone. He's what we need for this."
But Canot—mind, the lad had passed nineteen
A month before and all his life was fenced
By Salem, Smith's apothecary shop
And mucking in his mother's barn. How Bliss
Had found him there at Smith's behind his mortar
Is one for Bliss—he had a nose for men:
One look at Canot and that deviling eye—
Perhaps the way he pestled in the mortar—
One look was all that Bliss generally needed
Before the skinny beard wagged, making money,
And Canot listened to the tale of gold.
Whether he believed or not, who knows?
God knows, in Salem, back in the mid forties,
Young fellows wanting vessels had their pick
And Canot could have shipped a hundred times.
Why did he stick it, rolling pills and jujubes
And doing for his harridan old mother?
He was no fool. What's seagoing? Hard work,
Bad wages, loneliness, wet or dry rot, disease

And back to sea again after a fling!
Hadn't he seen it, even at nineteen!
And Canot never missed a thing he saw
Nor needed lessons twice. He signed with Bliss
As medical officer and the Captain's clerk.
This on a whaler, mind you, as though whales
Had poxes and the lad was out to dose 'em.
Well, Bliss filled Ames in, that you can be sure,
Between the time the sea chest went below
And Canot stood there on the quarterdeck
And says, "Quite ready, Captain. Shall we go?"
Ames looked him up and down. Old Crane had gone
Without a word. Bliss, spry as an old ram,
Jumped to the caplog from the quarterdeck:
"You have your orders, Captain Ames," he says:
"A full hold and a bounty for smart work."
He wags his beard once and starts up the wharf
While Ames pulls back those fat lips in a grin.
"We'll cast off, Mr. Canot, since you're here.
Now let go all!" The boatswain took it up
And the lines came in, sails tautened, her head swung
Into the stream.
    "Hope you'll like our whales,"
Ames says and hustles aft.
    The Indiamen
Were warped into the stream and had the wind,
The dock was clear but no one looked at her,
The HAPPY DELIVERY, another blubber trunk,
Another Newport scow shipped full of loafers.
No, not in Salem where the China trade,
Full-rigged barks and profits the same size
Made whaling riffraff traffic. No one looked,
And Ames swayed all up, let her take the wind
Running past Derby's Indiamen like a ghost.
Oh, she was an able vessel, something new
For those days, with a wicked rake to her bow
And masts that put her canvas in the clouds:

A witch for walking in those southern airs,
But stiff, too, mind you. When it came to blow
She'd set her rail down to it and go through
With that big everlasting leaded keel
Keeping her stiff and two hairs off the wind.
Not that Canot knew or cared. A ship
To him was only money under way;
But Ames, who'd had a dozen under him—
Blackguard, drunkard, scum of every dock—
He sailed the HAPPY DELIVERY with his blood
And when they took her from him he went mad.
Those southern passages were easy work
As those things went in those days. Dropping down
The latitudes from winter to the Line—
You've not forgotten it! The nights when fire
Flaked from the vessel's forefoot and new stars
Climbed up before you every southerly night.
A hard-bit lot, most of us sailors then,
But still we knew it, felt it, mostly at night
Or later, now, thinking and feeling back
As though you had a life nothing could touch.
And maybe that saves sailors at the last,
That innocence, for all the dirt they do.
But him? Not Canot. Whatever Canot was,
It wasn't seafaring, seamanlike or—able.
Oh, hard. He never had a seasick minute,
Could eat salt junk, spoiled beans, or live on air
And keep that dancing, mincing, sidelong gait,
That air that was a boy's—no age at all.
Whatever blew, Canot could trim to it
When others were hove down, as though his life
Had trained to that alone. On that first voyage
The HAPPY DELIVERY ran down the coast,
Her mastheads set with lookouts while the rest
Worked with the boatswain stowing stores below.
Stores! She shipped enough for ten year's found:
Barrels and hogsheads, boxes, bales, and kegs.

Why couldn't they have guessed? Oh every day
A masthead lookout hollered at a spout
And Ames would put out boats, and no one guessed.
They might have wondered when Canot took the cabin
Next to the skipper's and the mate moved out,
But you know sailors, how the day-to-day
Slips by in watches, deck work, trimming sail,
And nothing lives but ocean and this voyage.
Sailors don't ask until they leave the sea
And then—well, ask yourself: you just remember.

     Canot moved in. By day he kept alone
And set his medicines in racks, kept inventory
And spotted every cask or bale. Each day
He went down to the 'tween deck space and checked
The stowage. Not a stick could clutter space
If that were space for storage of whale oil.
He figured on a kill or two, though Ames
Was easy enough and didn't seem to mind
That boats put off for whales and never caught them.
He drove his vessel south with every rag
And he and Canot walked the deck at night
Or sat in the captain's cabin, where the lamp
Went out at dawn.
              They put in at Recife
For water. Ames let all hands go ashore
Except for one watch. Canot stayed aboard
Perhaps afraid of what he'd do—or spend!
But Ames, after his jokes about the brothels,
Went over the side—to see the owners' agents
He said with a leer, and Canot turned away
Not knowing Ames could sometimes tell the truth.

     When Ames came back to the dock with his new orders
He was half-drunk, having perhaps a sense
That such a voyage was mad, if lucrative.
At any rate, he went aft to his cabin

With Canot to read the orders. Can you see
The scene? The young man, hard with youth and Yankee,
Contemptuous of this drunken incompetent
Whom he could supersede (He'd plans for that!)
As for Ames, he thought he had a man
Who, dreaming for himself, would work for Ames.
Aft in the poop it was—a beam-to-beam
High-studded cabin built for a married man
With gilt-work in a frieze above the stern ports,
A table clamped to the deck and a single lamp.
The ports were open on the moonlit night
Giving across the water on the hush
And infinite barbarous stir of southern night.
They sat on either side of the vast table,
Canot with his orders and Ames slumped
Before his brandy bottle. As they sat
Motionless in the lantern-light, a wraith,
A slaughterhouse odor, like the sweat of marsh
Adrift in moonlight, stirred in the quiet room
And Canot twitched that peaked and foreign nose:
"Jungle swamps," he said, and read some more
While Ames, who knew that smell of old, said nothing.
You know it, eh? A middle-passage man
Must have it in his nostrils till he dies—
And after, too? Well, it's a thought to shrink
The skin across the back. I'll not forget
The first time when that stink was on my wind:
We were for ivory, coasting past Benin,
A black night with a gentle southerly air
With damp in it. All hands stayed topside then
To sleep. I woke. You'll tell me a plain smell
Along six miles of ocean air can't wake
A sleeping man. I'll tell you something evil
Brought me and all the new hands to the bulwarks:
It was as though the sea had running sores—
A sweet smell like a corpse or a newborn child:
I felt it like a grease on tongue and lips.

54

All of us younger hands looked at each other
And the boatswain grinned: "Slaver," he said. I looked
And saw the loom of a hull in a clearing patch
As the wind dropped and the air ran sweet again.
I learned to smell that smell for days and nights
Before I grew much older, but that first—
I know what Canot felt. Ames slumped down farther
And sipped his brandy. "Jungle swamps!" He laughed:
"A Portagee slaver, boy, and it's my guess
They'll have to burn her. She's too soaked with it."
Canot was looking from the wide stern ports;
The moonlight seemed to thicken. "I thought whalers
Stank bad enough. Thank God we're after whales . . ."
Ames laughed again. "You haven't read your lesson,"
He said and pointed. Canot held the sheaf
Of orders. Still he watched while the big ship,
A bark, four hundred tons at least, luffed up
And let go a bower with a roar of chain.
"Damned unpleasant neighbor," Canot said
And closed the ports. He sat and read again
While light seemed choked and oily, hard to burn.
A restless stir was afoot topside and Ames
Got up unsteadily. "You read ahead
While I take care of this." He stumbled out
And Canot heard him bawling for the boatswain,
Then heard a blow or two, one or two cries
And all fell silent underneath that stench.

  I suppose he learned to drink that night. You'll ask
If that was Ames's plan. The bottle stood
Under the lantern and he read the words:
"Make all maneuvers as for a whaling voyage
Until you reach Cape Verde. By this time stores
And water should be stowed, the 'tween-deck space
Compartmented with planking as provided,
And all trade-goods assembled as per invoice.
Prepared thus, you will head for the Gold Coast

Or Serralone, as seems most to our profit,
And treat with native rulers. We direct
As much avoidance of the Spanish, Portagee
And native factors as seems safe and wise.
DaSouza has great power on this coast:
If it should be his barracoons are full—
In which case, owing to the filth and plagues
He must lose all his stores—he will trade cheap.
However, deal with native potentates
Whenever possible. You may cruise south
As far as Bonny and New Calabar,
Keeping a close watch for the British cruisers
Said to be preying on legitimate trade.
In bargain, avoid expenditure of specie,
Be careful with your trade-goods, chiefly brass
And copper, but be prodigal with rum
The which, when peppered hot and of high proof,
Will prove most valued by the native kings . . ."
Canot went to the transom seat and flung
The ports wide open. In the oily moon
The slaver loomed, seeming between two lights
Of air and water, held up by her chain,
Aswim in fetor and corruption's glow—
The phosphorescent shining of decay.
He did not smell it now. The taste of brandy
Had cut the coating that had slimed his mouth
So he went back in and leaned above the paper:
". . . in our experience, severest losses
Have been incurred by carelessness in stowage,
Improvidence of rations, in neglect
Of proper cleanliness and exercise.
We therefore order that you feed your blacks
Twice daily, say at seven and at five,
At which times they shall use the jakes provided
And after this you shall enforce a rule
Of exercise. The blacks may be caused to dance
To drums, or judicious lashes will incite them.

They may do this two by two as they are fettered . . ."
He did not notice Ames beside him till
Ames laughed. "So, Mr. Canot, here's an end
To whaling—Well, I see you come to this . . ."
He heaved the empty bottle through the port
And the splash stirred sound and Canot smelled the night.
"You know the truth now. Here we are. At six
We point for the Cape Verde Islands. You can stay
Or we can leave you here, if this don't suit you."
There was an instant's silence. From the slaver
They heard a clank of iron and the splash
Of oars. "Unloading," Ames said. "Well, there's light
Enough for it."
            Canot turned a page
And read the last words: "Ships have come to grief
In many instances by incontinence
Of men and master. Hence our orders are
Against cohabitation with the women:
Many are poxy and it is well known
Their lustfulness is beyond our senses gross.
Therefore no fornications, no debauchery.
During the middle passage to Havana
You shall reserve your liquors, and no rum
Shall issue to the men lest it enflame
Their lust, relaxing discipline and thereby
Invite a mutiny, while it stains the soul.
In case of incapacity or death,
Command shall be assumed by Mr. Canot.
We wish you a happy, safe and prosperous voyage
And urge that you inform us frequently
Of your endeavors via homebound ships . . ."

It was then that Canot laughed, a cachinnation
The Greeks would call it. Did you study Greek?
Euripides met Canot several times
And they say that Athens rose on slavery . . .
I'm not drunk myself! That laugh of Canot's—

A tang of slaver in a human throat!
Ames turned on him: "For God's sake don't do that!"
But Canot looked out through the closed stern ports
Where on her cable the bark spread like a stain
And he laughed again. "Congratulate yourself"
He said. " 'A happy, safe and prosperous voyage' . . .
It will be prosperous, tell Bliss when you write
Of your endeavors—via homebound ships."
He turned and went out to the companionway
Turning before he climbed topside; "I learn
My lessons once, then better the instruction."
Old Ames leered at him, quite sober now,
While across the bay came jungle sounds and clash
Of iron on iron mixed with squalls of pain
As though the slaver's stink cried to the heavens,
Star-scattered, far, a jungle flecked with coin,
And Canot said, " 'Command will be assumed
By Mr. Canot' should you—have bad luck.
Luckily, I am here." He climbed topside
And Ames could hear his heels pound on the oak
Above his head, a threat in every stride,
Until the thick embracing southern night
Accomplished all and even Ames found sleep.

II.

Shift the decanter this way. That's good rum.
The stuff I've drunk to cure and drug my soul!
It goes down smoothly, tastes a bit like blood
And the best—like this—is black. You coasted Guinea
In the old days and know what rum is like—
You might say it made both of us—rum and blood—
Though nowadays it won't do to admit it
Since there are cleaner tools for dirty work
And all the slaves we sell are white and cheap:
It costs us nothing and they love their chains.
Or perhaps you think not? Then you're one of them!
Slavery's the worst, eh? Think it, then,

But you'll excuse me. No! to be enslaved
And never know it, count yourself a man
Fettered by brute necessity to job
And wife and household while the world
Wheels by you chiming the music of the spheres
And you deafened by iron clashed on iron!
Laugh if you want. Old men are old bad jokes
Told to the young who get the point when old,
And what's it all to us? The cat, rattan
Leg irons, brand and grating have all gone
With the skippers who used them into desuetude.
They did their work—we all did. Nowadays
The trade takes other passages. When it's time
To buy up bodies—and the time will come—
There will be Canots ready—Blisses too:
The world's agog with them.
                              That thought struck me hard
The day the world threw Canot at me, after
Some forty years, in a dockside tavern bar.
I'd put my vessel, a big iron bark,
In at a Baltimore pier to pick up hides.
My mate had stayed aboard and I went there
Into the tavern for a change of rum
And there he was. Oh, I didn't know him:
I'd sat at a table looking to the street
Watching the loaded drays clash past when someone—
A wraith, a dying flame at its last leap—
Stood smiling thinly at my side. "I'm Canot"
Was all he said. I set my glass down hard
And cracked it. "No, not a ghost. I thought I'd done it,
Outlived you all. Not you. You've got a ship . . ."
He looked across the street where the docks began
And I called for another glass. "Why not?" said Canot
Sitting across from me, not shaking hands.
I had not moved. The glass came, and a bottle.
"You needn't try to pretend you're glad to see me—
No. Stop. I want to know one thing. You're bound

For Boston. Will you take me? I've no money,
I can't pay. Just get me up to Boston
And I'll walk back to Salem and die there,
Not in this nigger country . . ." He trailed off
And I filled his glass. Looking at me he smiled
Boyish, ageless as ever. "I'd not ask it
Of a friend, if I had one and he were alive.
But of *you* . . ." I muttered something and he laughed
Canot's own laugh. "Always the owners' man,
Nose-led, middle-of-the-road. Oh never mind,
I get this way. I hate to beg, that's all."
Who would have dared to pity Canot? You?
No. You'd have been afraid. I was. I took him
Back to the ship. He'd nothing but himself
To stow aboard. I put him in my cabin
And—well, three days and nights till we raised Minot's,
Time enough to hear him out.
                                          That's the real rum,
Barbados, must be twenty over proof.
No, that's enough. You wanted Canot's story:
I come back there, to him. That's haunting for you,
As though his ghost, proper to Salem, came
And killed the town's luck with a poisoned breath
Stinking of rum and blood. At any rate,
Something killed Salem's trade and killed New England:
If Canot didn't, it was Bliss and Crane.
They made the customshouse by Derby Wharf
A monument to money long since gone
Or heaped in trusts for widows, spinsters, sons
Who leech on blood they'd never dare to drink.
Another curse for Salem. Drink to them all!
Lawrence Lowell Canot Cotton Mather:
A trinity with one substitute, in case
Someone discovers one has feet of clay.
No, don't mind me. It's off my chest. I know
It never weighted yours, and that's all right.

60

The run from Cape Verde to the Guinea coast
Was summer yachting to the HAPPY DELIVERY.
During the days of easy swells, the crew
Kept busy in the 'tween-decks setting up
Compartments. Ames had told all hands the truth
At last, one noon after the watch had changed,
He called all hands to muster by the break
At the poop. He stood up with the speaking trumpet,
Canot on his right a pace behind,
And put on the bluff and hearty seadog air
While Burns, the mate, who'd guessed it all along,
Stood with the men, his gaze fixed on the tops.
Canot had marked Burns as a man to go—
That busy head was wound up like a spring.
Well, Ames had his say: "If some of you still think
This vessel's after whales, you can think again.
Those try-pots forward ain't for melting blubber:
Some of you'll learn to cook up niggers' stew
And all hands better square theirself away
That there's been dirty voyages. I'll tell you
This one's a bugger. We're for Serralone
And the nigger barracoons along that coast.
We'll fill her full of blacks, then take the passage—
The middle passage west'ard to Havana.
If anyone don't like it, he can take
The deep six now, or when we get ashore
He can play bosun to some nigger king.
We're slavers now, boys."
                                            All the deck was still
Except for sea sounds, rig-and-tackle groans,
The wash of water travelling the hull,
And no one spoke, though several shifted feet
And looked at shipmates and then looked away.
"Mr. Canot here's in charge of trading parties,
Stowage and feeding. He'll say what he wants
And that'll be my orders. Mr. Canot . . ."

Ames left them then and there and went below
By the cabin scuttle. Canot stood alone,
Bent forward clutching the fife rail with both hands.
His face, with the dark eyes and the high-boned nose
Unweathered skin and red-lipped mouth like a burn
Hanging above the men as though a Fate,
An idol living by its own belief.
When he spoke his voice seemed high, far-off, a note
Familiar in the rigging, yet somehow changed,
And suddenly the men stirred. Burns looked down
And growled: "I never shipped to be no slaver."
A babble burst out. "Mr. Burns," said Canot,
"Control your men! I tell you and all hands
I shipped as you did, thinking to go whaling,
And found out later, just as you did now.
Good: the captain and the owners both
Have played their joke. Perhaps it's our turn now.
Because I swear I'll not go home tarred black
By Mr. Bliss's brush unless there's money
Enough to make all Salem kiss my hand.
What have *you* got to lose? You're dockside scum
Not fit to live ashore. And what's this life
At sea but slow death? Here's a chance to live.
With luck we can ship five hundred slaves . . ."

                                      A voice
Or two growled "Scum! Who's he calling scum,
That whitefaced storekeeper . . ."

                              Canot smiled at them;
His smile was vicious, opening the lips
like a rifle breech, and all was smooth, dark, oiled
For death.

            "I seem too young to take command
Of you like this? You, Mr. Burns, feel sore
Being set aside? Why bother? All I want
Is quick cheap barter for five hundred blacks,
A fast voyage to Havana, and my take.
Look at it like that. Now: any questions?"

A brief squall heeled the vessel down a moment
And they shifted, all but Canot who still held
The fife rail with a grip that showed his fear
Had any seen it. Oh, he was afraid:
Not of the men, the voyage, or what might come:
Of himself, I think, and what he'd found he was
When chance came naked to him, called his name,
And Canot was Chance's man.
                                        They all stood still
When the squall passed and with it words they might have said.
"Who's to see we get our share?" Burns said
And others took it up. Canot let go
The fife rail—he was sure now of himself—
"I'll see to it," he said. "If you don't trust me"—
He grinned like a dog at them—"and I can't blame you,
Why do as Captain Ames suggested, but
You might try trusting me to see this through,
And when we've sold our blacks you'll get your share.
I can't escape you, can I?"
                                        "I don't know."
Burns had stepped forward. "Sounds to me like mutiny.
Who's skipper here? Ames or you?" The growl
Of inarticulate assent went round the crew
And Burns spoke louder. "Ames and you get cash,
So much a head. What's the owners' share?
When all that's paid, how much is left for us?"
Canot bent over slightly, shifting his stance
As the vessel eased up in the lessening wind.
His red tongue flickered and he smiled again:
"Good questions, Mr. Burns. I think you know
The answers, too, since you have worked and sailed
For Bliss and Crane before. Perhaps you'll tell us . . ."
It was a stroke in the dark, accusing Burns
Of being Bliss's spy, the hired man
Keeping an eye on things. The men drew back
In a slight, vague retraction of themselves
And Canot saw it. "All of you know well

That I'm no seaman. I came on this voyage
As far as I knew, to be medical officer
And supercargo. Now we know we're slavers,
All of us. I'm to take care of *that* job.
Mr. Burns, you'll note the owners mentioned me
Though I am strange to them. They'll have their cut
After we see to ours. If they don't like it,
Let them find dirtier hands or cleaner work.
That's all. Now, who will stand with me in this?"
He stood erect and let his black eyes go
In slow arcs over every face before him
Until the ship's cook called out, "Bear a hand,
You swabbies. I got beans to cook. I'm with you."
And that was enough. Burns dismissed all hands,
Staying a moment to look up at Canot:
"You'll hang yourself, young feller." That was all
And Canot laughed. "Not till I've hanged some others,"
He said and turned back to the scuttle ladder
And dropped below.
              Just what was in that mind
He could not have said. Perhaps we can!
Surely the golden image had grown vast—
All capitalists begin with sensual images,
Images of what the stuff will buy:
The naked houri, the splendors of new senses,
The crowd's applause, rich, lovely nubile wives
And then the image peels down to the bones,
Strips off layers of fact, becomes a sign—
A symbol, you might say, of Power and Self.
Or taking the odd way, resolves to mere bank account.
But then, Canot was young and still had blood
So it's safe to say he'd peopled his head with girls
And what he'd do with them willing at night alone,
Or like his kind perhaps, dreamed they'd do the work
And play on his senses. Yet that Yankee thrift
Bridled the play of fancy, and the mind,
Forever whining to its spin, went round

The middle point: the power must be his.
Ames first, then Burns. And after that, the ship.
Or say, keep Burns to navigate and work
The vessel from Havana to New Orleans,
Then sell or burn her as luck seemed to offer
Or—try the Guinea Coast for another load!
His head was steaming with all this when Ames
Met him outside the cabin and pulled his sleeve:
"Come have a look at where we're going," he said
And pointed out his private chart, now pinned
To the cabin table.
          "Got a good fix this morning
And if this breeze holds, we'll be about *there*"—
He stabbed a sharp divider-foot—"By dawn.
That's Serralone, right here."
               Canot bent down:
He'd have to learn this navigating trick;
To keep Burns on was asking for betrayal,
But who would pilot the vessel? Think of the risks!
"What about cruisers?"
         Ames snorted, "Frigates! Scows!
None of them pungs could catch us, not this vessel,
Even if they found us with bare poles.
Worried about me?" Canot looked up and grinned.
"God, you're a dog," Ames said. "I heard you talk
The men around! With that crud-eatin' grin . . .
Why even Burns was like to sniff your tail . . ."
Canot was long past insult. He just laughed.

    That evening before sundown they saw sails
Lifting above the horizon to the south
And Ames piled on all canvas. Before long
The HAPPY DELIVERY was alone again
And it seemed that even then they could smell the land,
Or promise of a landfall may have flattered
Their senses and desire did the rest.
That night—like the last night before the Fall—

An air high up where the skysails gathered it
Impelled the vessel upright on her keel
As though a metal fragment sought the Pole.
Nature conspired with a Yankee trader
And even Africa, secret under dark,
Lay open, willing, while the ship bore down.
The men had come topside to sleep: the heat
Below decks drove them up. Gathered in knots
At the main chains, by the capstan, quiet and still
They waited, listening, sniffing the night
While under the southern coalhole, pit of black
Unstarred, the vessel swirled up flakes of light
That washed off aft and fell to dark again.

     Canot paced the quarterdeck alone:
Ames had joined him wanting to talk but Canot
Would take no gambit, so Ames went back below
To his brandy. Canot paced his back and forth
Athwartships, and the men could feel his stir
And wondered among themselves what restless ghost
Lived in his head. They didn't wonder much—
Sailors just don't. And who's to say they're wrong
To let the trouble slide until it's theirs
And all hands leap aloft, man guns, pass shot
Or powder? It's their business to turn to
And die, maybe. They know it comes to that.
On such a night, waiting for land to fall
Across their sense in a waif of scent from growth,
A rumor of breakers, a white line of surf,
They waited without anger or much hope,
Trusting in Canot if you call it trust
That says "Why not? He seems to know his business . . ."
They felt his unquiet spirit and were afraid,
In awe, and that felt better than despair.
If Canot knew that, he played up to them
But perhaps that's giving him the credit due to luck.
As you get older luck has more to say

Than the young will listen to, thinking as always
That bad luck is God's trick, good luck their own
Divine capacity, their loveable
And fine-drawn soul exacting its just due,
A gift free-given them but rightly theirs.
Young men expect good luck and call it virtue:
Old men make sacrifices, pray the god,
And if they luck it out, they are not happy,
Only relieved. They wait for the next time.

If I read Canot right, his head was full
Of more than images now: he'd tasted power,
The metal taste that comes from running hard.
He knew men bent before his will. The sergeants
And petty officers rest content with this,
Though the real masters never are so sure
And each day train the muscle of the will
To prove their potency. Lechers of ambition
Or self-deception—it's the same at last
Or was with Canot. Putting dreams aside
He went up forward to the men and gave
His orders for the working-party schedules.
It was all cut and dried: each boat would have
A boat commander, coxswain and four oarsmen
And all were to be armed with knives and carbines.
He'd picked his men: one was Ned Bouguereau
Who later sailed with Semmes in the ALABAMA,
Went up through the hawsehole to commissioned rank
Before he took to opium out Chinaside.
He was a boy then but the hardness showed.
Canot gave him the longboat to command
Figuring he was one to stand no nonsense
From black or white. Well, all that night he drilled them:
He split them into watches, to be guards
At the ladders, to keep the niggers quiet.
Funny how you can lose the rights and wrongs
Of anything in pure technique. The men

Might as well have trained for coast-guard work,
For a game, repelling Huns or playing store!
They lost themselves—I mean that word for word—
They lost all moral being in Canot's planned
And private world. Slaving with a vengeance!

By dawn the 'tween-deck spaces, boats and gear
Were ready for the trade. As light came up,
A florid sunburst level with the bow,
The lookout hailed a landfall. Dead ahead
They saw the surf-line, darkness at its back,
And they knew their time had come, or Canot knew it.
Ames came on deck, part sober: he was drunk
Or halfway shot all night and half the morning,
And Canot turned away from him, unshaven
And crumpled, stinking of rotten teeth and brandy.
Why not? Would you salt mines or juggle books
Or float fake companies without morning clothes?
People can't be conned by sodden tramps—
Not that a Canot makes slave-trading decent,
But if the folks at home will have their slaves
They want their slavers sober, clean, and smart,
Like rising bank clerks—oh, very well then, say
Like a ship's officer: that's one for me.

III.

By Sherbro Island, where the Sherbro River
Comes down to sea, there is an open sound.
You know those coasts: Gold, Grain, Slave, Ivory,
The Bight of Benin and its evil waters,
A thousand miles of surf, all harborless
With neither curving arms of land to shelter
Your vessel from the sea, nor holding ground
A hook can fasten in. How many bowers,
Cables, shackles, men and ships lie there
Under the final sea that finds us all!

Small wonder that DaSouza's barracoons
Were busiest at Sherbro, where the islands
And inlet give a vessel peace. DaSouza
Made millions by that fact until the British
Put cruisers on the coast to kill the trade.

    Bliss had ordered Ames to trade direct
With native kings—DaSouza's prices cut
The profit far below what Bliss thought reasonable
But Ames knew better: if the British cruisers
Were in the way, DaSouza's barracoons
Would be full up with drafts from Dahomey,
Up-country tribes and local prisoners.
That being so, DaSouza could not keep them
For long, with plagues, short rations and rebellions.
So if a vessel, able fast and smart,
Got in, could take five hundred or so blacks
Before the cruisers knew, he would sell cheap
Or never sell at all. The HAPPY DELIVERY
Could take her full load here, all in two days,
Be up and away on the middle passage west
Instead of sneaking up and down the coast
And chaffering with villainous black kings.
This was Ames's plan. He had told no one
But stood in, on that morning, close aboard
Great Turtle Island. Not a sail in sight
And on the mainland beach only a still
And upright spire of smoke behind some palms
Told of the hid stockade, the barracoon.
All hands were on deck. Up into the wind
And the anchor dropped—Ames kept it at short stay
To bring in fast, or slip, in case of cruisers.
He put two lookouts to each top and set
An anchor watch, put Burns in charge with orders
To fire a round from the long gun in the stern
If the lookout sighted sails, or to shift ground
If the anchor dragged, keeping inshore

So that from seaward nothing of the ship
But blended into surf, trees, hill, and sand.

Ames took Canot to the rail: "We'll take
The longboat in and see what we can do.
If DaSouza's got the blacks and wants to trade
We'll make the deal. And then you go to work.
I hope he's got some prime black girls," he added
And leered at Canot. "Each of us gets their pick
Of two, you know—you and me and Burns."
He laughed as Canot drew off from him scowling.
"You wait, boy. Dark meat's tasty after seagoing."
He laughed again while Canot walked away
And spoke to Ned Bouguereau who was standing by
The longboat, ready with a brace of pistols,
A cavalry carbine and a bayonet
Cut down to a dirk thrust in a scarlet sash:
Even real killing was a game to Ned.
They lowered away with Ned inside the boat
Riding the sternfall, easy as any gentleman
Astride his mare before the morning's hunt.
Down went the Jacob's ladder and a coxswain
Scrambled aboard followed by two oarsmen.
Then Canot swayed down and last of all went Ames
A touch precariously, having primed himself
With a double jolt of brandy.
                              They shoved off
And made for the mouth of the swirling Sherbro River,
Swift-running red between two juts of land:
The blue, heaving swell, the surf to right and left,
Ahead the land, still black in early light
And dead ahead of them the red-run stream.
Meanwhile no stir or signal came from shore:
The plume of smoke stood up in the still air,
A fume of swamp drawn up by warming sun
Hung in a haze that veiled the hills behind
And nothing betrayed itself. The longboat moved

With a creak of tholepins and a swash of water
Strict to a purpose needing speech nor sign
As from the misted hills two vultures came,
Two kites that drifted in ascending steam
Above the smoke plume from the hid stockade,
And "Way enough," the coxswain said. The oarsmen
Shipped oars. The boat's stern grated on the sand.
Bouguereau, on the bow thwart, jumped ashore
Holding the painter. As he hauled it in
And the others leaped from the bow thwart to the beach,
A stranger, in white European clothes,
Came from the scrub palms at the edge of sand
And stood, a long cheroot cocked in his teeth,
To watch what he must have watched a hundred times.
You knew DaSouza in the old days? No,
He must have taken his fortune back to Paris
By your time. Well, you missed a trick. DaSouza
Was what you'd call a wholesaler, I suppose—
Had factories and barracoons from Sherbro
Almost to Gran' Bassam and Abidjan,
With factors working for him inland up the rivers,
At least before the British went to work
In earnest. When they did, DaSouza quit,
Picked up his earnings and went off to Paris,
Leaving the native kings with stock enough
To keep them in human sacrifice for years.
I used to see DaSouza in the old days—
He liked young men! "My dear boy," he would say
When I looked askance at him and his dirty business:
"The kings and medicine men would kill the creatures
And eat them. When I sell them off to you
My dear boy, they have at least a chance—
Ah, don't ask; chance for what? You rather sound
Like an English humanitarian liberal . . ."
(Pointing to a pile of new-minted titles
On a walnut table looted out of Florence)
"Such nasty folk, these lovers of their fellows.

Most of them kill or beat their wives and children
While seized with paroxysms of philanthopy."
He'd sip his oloroso, heave a sigh, then leaning forward
Would pat the inside of your leg and say, "My dear,
One has to face facts, which are never nice:
One's born unpleasant in an unpleasant world,
And in my own case, with expensive tastes
That take some gratifying. I sell slaves
To those who want them. I get them from their rulers.
In more enlightened countries, subjects go
To die in armies and the corpses rot.
Here, they sacrifice them to the juju
And after, eat them. The rest they sell to me
To sell to you to sell to Cuban planters
Who grow this fine tobacco I'm so fond of.
It's no use telling me the blacks are human:
Of course they are. So, I believe, are your
American Indians. They are in your way
And must be killed. The blacks are my investment
Cropped out here under all-wise Providence
And I serve economic law, demand,
Supply and M. DaSouza. Let that be
A lesson to you." Then he would lean back
And suggest some—recreation for that night.
I can imagine Canot, who was young,
Good-looking and not quite the finished work
He later made himself, taking that in!
For Ames was right: the barracoon was full
And DaSouza had despaired of trading vessels
To buy up his supply.
                              Canot and Ames,
Finding DaSouza there on the beach beside them,
Began to talk together, though Ames
Stumbled over his tongue from drink and exertion
And Canot did the talking. That would have been
A scene to witness; the boats drawn up, the men
Uneasy, except Bouguereau, with their hands

Nervous at the gunstocks, and those three
In casual parley as though on a city street,
Between the white surf and the jungle green
While over them all, the finest work of nature,
The unequivocal equatorial sun
Drew shadow up like water into cloud.
Canot arranged it all: DaSouza saw
Where business lay and took them to his house,
Though Canot kept Ned Bouguereau for a bodyguard,
Leaving the rest to watch the boat. The heat
Poured out of sky, rebounding from the sand,
Turned off as a valve shuts when the jungle
Closed in around them, following a path.
They moved in a slow incline away from sea,
Away from the barracoon, though as they walked
A shout or two, a hubbub of crowded life
Pressed in, receded, and Ned Bouguereau
Shifted his carbine. Up in front DaSouza
Half turned his head. "It's feeding time. I trust
You gentlemen will take them all. I've food
For another day or two on hand, and then—"
He turned his head back. "We'll take all we can,"
Said Ames and laughed. The laughter rang out harshly,
Then quenched in growth and silence. No one spoke
Again until they stepped out into sun
Onto a lawn, a vista and a grove
Where at the center, at a fountain's foot,
A huge flamboyant, like a thousand flames,
Burned living red before them. Gentle slope
Gathered the eye and led it to a knoll
Where a white bungalow with low-lying wings
Spread on the crest. It promised coolness, shade
Of awnings spread and jalousies and sounds
Of water racing from a far-off height.
They walked in, leaving Bouguereau outside
On the wide veranda, plunging into dark
And the cool murmur of DaSouza's talk

Mingled with the sounds of running stream
And the icy ticking of an unseen clock
Before their eyes could find light in that shade.
Shapes came before them, and DaSouza's voice
In an alien sound set several shapes astir
And Ames and Canot found themselves in chairs
Low and caressing. Then as their eyes found light—
The motion of the sea still in their heads
And bodies—light was gathered and they saw
DaSouza smiling while a young black girl
Held glasses on a tray, bowing before them.
"You do yourself pretty well," said Ames and drank
While Canot kept his eyes away from her,
The girl, who moved across his sight and left
A swirl of air about him.
                              It was then
DaSouza spoke of business, after Ames
Had found the bottom of a quart and sleep.
Canot had forced himself to state his terms
Though the oloroso had racked him between sleep
And succulent images of the girl. He spoke
Deliberate Yankee while DaSouza smiled,
Agreeing to the trade, and they shook hands.

    Canot left Ames and went back to the ship
Having promised DaSouza to return by sunset.
DaSouza was too old for sport himself
But—there was Canot. And that alone was sport,
To throw him fish and watch him dive. Remember,
I gave DaSouza sport, too. He enjoyed it.

    IV.

    When the sun went down and a breeze came off the sea
DaSouza took them down to the barracoon
With Bouguereau and a dozen household slaves
As guards. The evening spread out cool and still
Smelling of blossom, earth, and hardwood smoke

As they passed between the mangrove swamps and forests
Devouring daylight to make darkness fat.
Beyond the trees lights wavered and the hum
And hubbub of the barracoon grew louder.
Who knows what pictures streaked through Canot's head?
Had he ever known nights like this, or dreamt of darkness
As fecund, moist and rotten? he was young:
Blood will swell and darken in young men
At nightfall, when all's strange and nature whispers
"God is not here, or if He is, He winks."
A changed world where blood beats to another tune.
Somewhere beyond sight the vessel lay
With rig and tackle purposed to their end
And beyond her, Cuba, Salem, Bliss, and Crane—
Incurious, hard and moral as a coin.
You shift in your chair, remembering. You've known
Too many go bamboo or Asiatic
To laugh. I've felt those evenings, warm as wombs,
Around me, as though all the earth were loin,
Mysterious interstice dark with growth.
A man goes once too often to that source,
Gives and goes in to the open yielding cave
Of tropic night just one more time too often . . .
Perhaps you say that you and I escaped
As Canot did. I think not. That embrace
Breeds anguish in the vein and nerve forever,
An ache about the groin, and in the guts
A fire that eats you out with lechery—
Or bursting out, consumes men, nations, land,
Black blood like lava killing where it runs.

 The high stockade, DaSouza's barracoon,
Spread out in a clearing. At DaSouza's word
The guards unlocked the gate and they went in
On hard-packed earth. A hundred fires burned
Ringed round by Negroes, bound with sisal cords.
DaSouza sniffed the air. "Still sweet enough.

You came in time to reap a healthy crop."
Canot, within that circle, saw at last
The goods he bargained for. The singing and movement
Had died as the white men entered the stockade,
And about their fires, swept in and out of shadow,
By gusty flames, the Negroes looked away
And in their quiet and removal seemed
An inert patience waiting for its trial.
DaSouza slipped his hand under Canot's arm:
With Ames and Bouguereau and a guard of blacks
Behind, they strolled the long perimeter
Past knots of women, children, girls, and boys.
In the shifting firelight DaSouza's form
In white showed brilliantly or rinsed with shade
And Canot felt the fingers on his arm
And heard the immaculate voice like a cicerone's.
The thing was settled: in a nice accord
Of goods and money, they had made the price:
As soon as light allowed, the HAPPY DELIVERY
Would stand close in, and dugouts, the ship's boats
And makeshift rafts would load the blacks on board.
"There'll be no trouble," said DaSouza, halting
Before a fire where a group of women,
One suckling an infant, looked at him
And turned away. "They've nothing worse to fear
Than their own kin and the magicians of their tribe . . ."
Canot looking down where one girl lay
Asleep or so it seemed, one leg drawn up,
The torso straining back and the dim breasts
Awash in light and shade like a pulse of blood,
Flickered his tongue along his drying lips.
"I've seen enough," he said. A pace behind
Ned Bouguereau spoke, Ames's laugh rang harshly.
On the ground the sleeper stirred—
Her eyes opened, clear, unwinking, calm
To take him in. The fingers on his arm
Released, then tightened. DaSouza too looked down.

"We'll make smart work to get them all aboard,"
Said Canot, as the girl rolled on her side,
The head turned and the brief skirt pulling up
Set Canot's tongue a-flicker. "As you wish,"
DaSouza said. "I've no reports of cruisers
Closer than Bonny. You may take your time.
Though of course being new out here and in the trade,
You may well feel some apprehension." Canot
Looked up at him. "Do come back to my house.
I hope you'll stay the night. For all the rigors
Of a primitive life, I've some amenities
To offer . . ." Canot looked away. The girl
Had made no further move. It came upon him,
Seeing her waiting there for someone's need,
That this was his. The fire on the ground
And in his skull trembled and beat. DaSouza
By gentle pressure led him to the gate
And as they came out into fallen dusk
DaSouza said, "I'd had my eye on her.
I'll have her brought to the bungalow after dinner;
She might amuse you . . ."

            For the next three hours
Canot turned on a spit, tried out and fired.
DaSouza, knowing how to find his fun
In savage remote corners, found in Canot
An extended joke. New England guilt and youth.
Knew? of course he knew! In a few hours
DaSouza had found more of Canot out
Than Canot knew was there. Not the first time
A Yankee trader'd come to bring home money
In all sweet chastity. Canot was nineteen.
Nineteen! Imagine that, then see yourself
All at once nineteen, a Salem boy
Got somehow behind God's back to find the laws
Of white New England spitted on the equator
And sweating their drop by drop over tropic heat.
DaSouza watched him shifting in his chair

While dinner lasted. Bouguereau had gone
Long since to the servants' quarters for his game,
The bottles were three deep by Ames's place,
And that worthy, knowing that once at sea
There'd be enough dark meat but no more sherry,
Had plumped for DaSouza's finest oloroso
And slept a well-earned sleep. DaSouza poured
Himself a glass of port and tried a story
Of youthful exploit on his guest, amused
By these odd Yankees and their sensual thrift.
"And that, my dear, is why I've not gone home—
Apart from the money, as you can understand.
For a young man it's a life of risk and chances
But much more satisfactory. So I stayed.
Now that I'm old, or very nearly so,
I think of settling down, in France for choice,
And marrying a comfortable youngish person . . ."
Canot listened at first. The older man
Had told, most elegantly, of bloody fights
Upriver, stealing blacks, and how that violence
Had worked solution in debauch at night
With troops of slave-girls from the barracoons,
The inexhaustible heats by blood engendered,
The liquors, potions—you have heard them all,
Those tales, and their sequels not so often told
Of middle-passage vessels when all hands
Went mad at the touch of alien flesh and blood.
Then on that night, when even from the house
They could hear the stirring in the barracoon,
Old tales ran lively along Canot's veins
And all he saw was the deep shadowy secret
Of the black girl's eyes, the slow coil of her loins
In motion, turning on her side.
DaSouza may have planned to talk religion—
He did that with his victims at such times—
But then dismissed the thought. "My dear," he said,
"You show a fine New England sense of breeding

To listen to an old man half the night.
Allow me to arrange for Captain Ames
While you pursue youthful pursuits, whatever
The house affords. I might," he added slowly
As Canot wrenched his chair back and half-rose
To go, he couldn't have said where, "explain that I
Have ordered that black girl whom I think you noticed
To be sent up here. If that sort of thing
Would entertain you, please feel free to use
The rooms out there . . ." he gestured to the rear.
Canot stood up. A tall Negro slave
Had entered. DaSouza spoke in an unknown tongue
And the Negro bowed. "Forgive me if I stay
Alone here for a time. You younger fellows
Can bolt your pleasures and digest with ease
But I, being old, must savor as I can.
If you'll just follow Pablo, you will find
Matters as well arranged as I can manage.
I'll look in on you later, if I may . . ."
The Negro Pablo, signalled by the pause
In his master's discourse, turned and Canot followed
In just what dream of mingled lust and terror
I leave you to imagine. We can leave
DaSouza in a welter of delight,
Of laughter, the vicarious elderly reprise
Of sense departed, drinking and imagining,
While through the long low-studded shadowy rooms
The Negro padded, thinking what you and I
Could not have known then, though today we guess.
He showed him to a door that led to a wing
Back from the house, half-hidden in bamboos
And strange hardwoods. Bowing once, he left
And Canot walked with his shadow down a hall
Lit only by a dim moon through the lattice
Clacking in rhythm with the bamboo limbs
While all about him crowded a press of life
Unseen, not understood, half-threatening.

Ahead, another door, a slat of light,
Across which once a shadow licked a tongue,
Lay open. What would you have felt? I know
What I would feel—remember, I was there
And knew DaSouza, though at twenty-three
I'd known some women—not enough to count
By sailors' standards, but compared to Canot
I was Don Juan. But then, I'm not from Salem,
Or by adoption only. Ah, these foreigners!
Poor moth, he drifted toward that streak of light
Making a soft whisper with his feet
On the cocoa matting. His heart skipped when some beast—
A lizard perhaps—skittered along the roof.
But he came there at last, to the door ajar
And crossed the threshold. All he saw at first
Was a window open and latticed, half-astir,
Two bamboo chairs, a dresser with a glass
Aswim with shadow. There was no one there—
Not by the bed, wide, high, and looped with gauze—
No one at all. He looked while nothing stirred
But the flame of the oil lamp in the far corner
And nothing sounded but the pulse of night,
Then walked another step inside until
He put his right hand out to grasp the bedpost,
Turning to look inside the net that stretched
From the ceiling down, a soft cone vague and hiding.
She lay there facing him as she had lain
Before in firelight, with one leg drawn up
And the eyes bright black-and-white, wide as mirrors;
He could but think she knew, had known and wanted
What he desired, seeing her first that evening,
And come of her own free will and free desire.
He might have called it love. He was the kind
To call it love, thinking that made it clean.
Perhaps young fellows do that the first time
And afterward know better, or don't care
Seeing the world goes on as it did before

For all they've plowed new pastures and made hay.
The tales I've heard—and told—of the first time!
All romances, lies, mere growings-up
Or harkenings-back to what they wished had been
Instead of that ineptitude, that grappling,
Handmade anticipation broke by fact!
Ah well, I agree: young men are fools, old men
Are—old.
          Canot was young. He'd drunk enough
To swallow Salem like a pill. The room,
The night, the sense of distance from the world
Gathered like light into those gazing eyes,
And as he stood upon their brink, she moved
In a single motion starting at the loins
That writhed him in, a part of her reclaimed.

       Waking at dawn, a heaviness upon him
That made him turn to her for ease, he found
The impress of her body there but she
Was gone. He started up. DaSouza sat
By the window, smiling at him, a cigar
In his long white fingers.
                 "Such a peaceful sleeper,
My dear boy. It's a shame to waken you.
But business being business, Yankees being Yankees,
I felt you'd best be up and stirring, rather
Than cope with conscience's reproach all day."
Canot pulled his clothes on. He was naked
And hated being seen that way. DaSouza,
Who guessed as much, just looked him up and down
And asked him if he'd slept well, had enjoyed
The freedoms of the house, with one or two
Comments on the whiteness of the skin,
The breadth of shoulder, straightness of the legs,
And Canot blushed all over, could not speak
Remembering the night, flushed with success,
Desire, rage, and just a trace of guilt

While DaSouza added, "The girl had to leave
Before dawn broke. She didn't really want to
But I persuaded her . . ."
                                    "You mean you've been here . . ."
"Oh, quite some time, my dear. I sleep so poorly,
And then an old man likes to see the young
Enjoying themselves. It rather renews one's youth
Without the labor and expense." He rose:
"We'll meet again on the beach before you go,"
He said and walked out waving his cigar,
While Canot, left alone, knew then that though
Last night had passed in darkness, there were two
Who knew him now. He'd given himself away
And the world should pay for that. It was no gift.

V.

   Down by the barracoon Bouguereau waited
With the working parties. Canot, self-possessed
And cold, came along the path and looked them over,
Ran them through the procedure and turned them to
With Bouguereau in charge. Beyond the line
Of palms that screened them from the sea, the ship
Was standing by, her anchor at short stay
While her boats in cadence walked the water in
Toward shore, each breaking out a plume of white
At her forefoot. Canot sent Bouguereau
Back to the beach to keep the boats in order
While he himself went into the stockade.
Inside, the fires were out. The blacks in groups
Of four or six, stood bound with sisal, withes
And bits of rag while DaSouza's native guards
Stood by or pricked the laggards with their spears.
At the front of the compound were the men, the women
And children at the rear and out of sight
As Canot with a guard of four armed sailors
Walked in. Was he afraid? Were you? Was I
Afraid in those days? Five hundred strapping blacks,

Three hundred men and fifty half-grown boys:
We learned to be afraid, and so did Canot.
Yet even then as he strode, or call it walked,
On the iron-hard dirt flattened by lives and deaths
Beyond his counting—even then he feared.
For what? Lest he should see his last night's growth
Before him in that girl? And even then,
It came to him that he was changing, changed
By the trade, the darkness calling to the dark
Inside and breaking into flesh and feature.
He hoped he would not see her, hoped he would,
Feared this stranger she had made of him.
Yet all the while, as the blacks filed toward the boats,
He checked them off against DaSouza's invoice.
Then, as it came the women's turn, he sent
For Bouguereau and handed him the list
And went to the shore and took the dingy out.
Back on board, he stood by the main hatch aft.
Boats came alongside—rafts, dugouts deep
And sluggish with their loads. They tumbled up
On deck by scores all morning, mostly men
And boys, and as they came across the bulwarks
The shipfitter ironed them two by two at wrist
And ankle and armed men thrust them down below.
Below! I think Hell tiers us up like that,
Or will when our time comes. I went below
In a Spanish bark once, somewhere off Calabar,
And saw . . . You don't need telling. Under way
For three or four days I suppose she'd been.
You know those Spanish barks, with bluff high sides
And lofty overheads in the 'tween-deck space.
They'd rigged, between the orlop and the maindeck,
Two stowage decks with three feet clearance each
And there the niggers lay, some side by side
Manacled together by arm and leg,
While some, with collar and chain fast to a cable
Running the length of the hold and bolted down,

Were stacked up sitting in each other's laps
Like chairs in a ballroom when the party's over.
They'd had no sloppy weather yet. The decks
Were clean enough. A windsail swept in air
Through open hatch and ports—all tight and shipshape.
The HAPPY DELIVERY was none of those
Broad-beamed, high-sided, bluff-bowed, roomy tubs
But a fore-and-main topsail schooner, sharply built
With little freeboard and a steep deadrise
That made her weatherly and fast but cramped
Even for her crew. Well, Canot loaded
Five hundred or so blacks between the keel
And topsides—laid them end on, side by side
On flanks with each man's crotch in the next one's bum
Or on their backs in rows, feet touching feet.
He'd worked it out—had drawn himself a sketch,
Noted the dimensions of each hold,
The cubic feet of slave each hold allowed
And sent them down. The carpenter had rigged
A cable, rove through ring bolts, passing through
The thwartships bulkheads. Every man was tied
To a fellow and this cable. Canot's plan
Allowed for feeding them below at dawn,
And in the afternoon for taking sets
Of fifty or a hundred up topside
Where the cooks would have the try-pots full of stew,
The jakes would be set up for men and women,
And the happy savages after food and function,
Could dance on the decks from natural high spirits.
Canot would see they danced: with exercise,
Good food, and cleanliness, this bumper crop
Would make it to the market, if *he* knew!
They came in over the side, silent, cold.
The crewmen and coxswains, cursing at the landing
And ladders, prodded the laggards up with boat hooks.
Oh they lost a couple. One lad came aboard—
A straight, tall fellow about Canot's age,

A face like a mask with vivid eyes, reminding
Of other eyes. Canot met these an instant,
Then turned away. The lad stood on the bulwarks,
As though alone, though ironed to another,
An oldish, stooped, washed-out looking nigger
With that tubercular pallor . . . Well, he stood there
And Bouguereau, from the ladder, pricked his thigh
With his dirk. The fellow half-turned, kicked at Ned,
Then dragging the other with him, threw himself
Into the sea. They sank without a bubble
In ten or fifteen fathoms. After that
Canot set men to see the blacks moved fast
Over the bulwarks and across the deck.
A prime young fellow lost was a fat sum
What with the price of field hands in New Orleans.
As for a child or two who missed their footing
And tumbled over—sharks took care of them.
I don't say Canot liked all this. He stood
And tallied them all, while Ames stayed in his bunk.
What battled in his veins? After the men
Were stowed and ironed in the lower spaces
The women came aboard. Ned Bouguereau
Had plucked the girl out from the wailing throng—
The women keened, a nasal lasting note
Like a hurt dog's, though all the men were silent—
And sent her to Canot's cabin under guard
So Canot did not see her come aboard.
He felt regret, yes. What would you have felt
At nineteen? Canot must have sensed that now,
With DaSouza left behind, Ames gone bamboo
And nothing but sea and sky to check his will,
That he had but to loose his hand and power
Would fall; to clench it, and his hand was power.
He kept his eye on the tally sheet and saw
Only the splayed feet go past. And though
His blood beat hot and swift behind his eyes—
Drenching him with images of last night

Sounding along the corridors of his head
Bull-roarings like the minotaur's of rage,
Regret, despair, imprisoned in strange flesh—
He kept his tally in a clerkly hand.
They did not stop to eat or rest. The boats
Plied from the beach. Canot looked up once
Or twice toward shore and still the black thread ran
From the barracoon through scrub palms to the beach
As white in sunlight as a folded wave.
"Drive 'em" was all he said and all that day
They drove them, all hands bowed to it, oar and line,
Boat hook and maul, like all the sons of Noah,
Though Burns kept lookouts, each for an hour's trick,
At fore and maintops. One sang out at noon
And Burns slipped up aloft with the Captain's glass:
It might have been a cruiser, but she faded
To westward out of sight, and Canot drove them.
By five o'clock the hold was full. The beach
Lay chaste and empty under lengthening light
And as a brace or two of youngish women
Came over the side and Canot marked them down,
Ned Bouguereau pushed his hat back, wiped his hands
Across his thighs, and "That's it, Mr. Canot,"
He said and grinned: "Let joy be unconfined.
The fun's beginning." Canot stretched his lips
A little. "Mr. Burns!" Burns came to him
Pushing through the queues formed by the hatch.
"Weigh anchor and sway up. We'll be going now . . ."
He would have turned away, but Burns stood still:
"I want the Captain's orders, Mr. Canot."
And Bouguereau grinned again. "He's drunk below,"
He said. "I don't believe you'd get your orders."
"That'll do, Bouguereau"—Canot grinned too—
"We'll work on out of here, I think. The owners,
If you remember, Mr. Burns, named me
As Captain Ames's standby. Take the deck
At once." Burns looked at Bouguereau and shrugged,

86

Then called the boatswain. All the boats were in,
Made fast and stowed. The boatswain's call squealed out
And men went aloft or forward to the windlass
To heave in on the single bower cable
While over them sails bellied between yards,
The fore and main booms swung to gather air
And jibs flew fluttering, till, sheeted in,
They found an unseen purchase, the ship edged forward
Breaking the anchor's hold. They were under way.
Canot went aft and from the taffrail looked
Off eastward to the shore, the curve of beach
Where Sherbro runs in red between two arms
And saw a single figure, hand upraised
As though in benediction. But DaSouza
Was not that sort. It must have meant "farewell"
And Canot might have thought he saw that smile
Remembering last night. Then he turned away,
The image of the girl, of night, the netted bed,
DaSouza by the window: Canot clenched
His fist and struck the rail and hurt himself
So that the pain might blur those images.
The HAPPY DELIVERY, swung clear of the islands,
Low in the water and her head turned west,
Was walking on a perfect compass bearing
And Canot swallowed twice and went below.

VI.

First light at morning, sun against your back,
An albatross high and slant across the dawn,
Fresh on the planking a delicate sweat of night
And the first stir of turn-to: though a ship
Stand out for war, new latitudes, slaves, gold
Or just the future, dawn makes all the same—
New-washed, delivered out of darkness, vessels
Salute the morning, innocent and fair.
I can see you stir to that, remembering,
How it all tasted on the eye, skin, tongue

With salt and fresh together, rivers of tide
And ocean-seeking water at the flood!
Perhaps thinking of Canot, you'll allow
A portion of such delight even to him.
The breeze was fresh. Wind sails curved out hard
And shunted air below. He sniffed the morning
And stretched. Around him vastness fell away
Beyond imagining; had he such a mind
He might have thought of all the life below
Packed like a cinder in the eye of God—
Himself a Noah, containing worlds, while flood
Ran all about him miles and days of arc.
He went to the main hatch and the man on watch
Slid back the cover. There was life down there.
A wraith of odor. Sounds as of a monstrous growth
That fed on dark and fattened, bursting its shell.
Canot moved away, the hatch slid-to,
And the HAPPY DELIVERY spoke again in bubble
Of moving water, wind and standing rigging.
A wordless, uncompanionable noise
To him, who was alone. Let all stay so.
He was no sailor and a sailor's ghosts
Would never haunt him—not like you and me
Who wake at night, a thousand miles of land
Turning us while we lie there and smell salt
Or hear in morning traffic the groan of shrouds
And for that instant, crowded as a grave,
All oceans claim us. Ghosts moving among ghosts,
Poor landlocked sailors, old, rich, crammed with our sins
But innocent when we can smell the sea.
Could Canot sniff it through that fleshless nose?
A whiff might come there, but it stirred no nerve,
Made nothing leap up warm about his heart
As a hull leaps to the eye above horizon.
He was alone, I tell you. All that night
He'd done what DaSouza might have hoped for him—
What an addition to DaSouza's tales

Of Yankee traders, after he'd done with them!
Why tell it? It's a tired enough story
To us who've seen and known—maybe forgot
At times, a little while. When we go bad
It's longer and steeper down and the way back
Is for a few. New Englanders don't damn
The easy way. We make our minds up to it
And take the deep six open-eyed, with lead
We've molded to the heart to keep us down.
I like that! What, be damned and never know it
Till God winds on the bullhorn and the word
Gets passed for quarters, all ye happy saved?
Give me the man who knows and pays his price
And asks no snivelling forgiveness after!
I don't mean Canot. All that was all lies
To him. If he'd been born among the blest,
He'd have seen hypocrites and dirty linen:
"Power," he'd say. "The others think they have it
But they don't know. I do, and that's my chance . . ."
He thought like that, you know. On this first morning
Of the middle passage, he was chance's man.
The night before, he'd gone down to the girl,
Taking a bottle or two of Ames's brandy,
And sat her on his lap beside the table
While he poured it down her, taking a few himself.
God! I don't imagine you can see it
And better so. I don't suppose the girl
Had ever tasted brandy. Canot talked
Sitting there in the chair below the lamp,
The stern ports open to the groping wind.
He talked about himself, said everything
As over a calm water the vessel walked
A white track to the westward, a long line
Marking the sea an instant. Canot spoke
His mind—his soul, if you prefer the term—
Talked out his secret, finding it with words.
She had found him out. Let her know it all:

Let darkness, the sea, this passage out of night
Into the mystery of hidden ends—let them all speak.
What did he do to her? As the steering cables
Groaned on the blocks, as the wake drew aft
And night sounds, deck sounds, sounds of a life apart
Drew round the vessel, an uncertain world,
Canot worked out his vengeance. I could tell you
What he told me: how he marked her with his hate,
His secret perhaps. Canot is in his grave
And the girl's flesh, wherever it went, is free of him.
I'll say no more of that. Nature has its limits
And nature's hold on Canot was precarious.
How much of him have we . . . Well, that's best dropped!
Canot could find pleasure where you and I
Would vomit. He had not forgot that night
In DaSouza's house: she was the one who knew
The worst of Canot. Since she knew it all
Then let it mark her, with his mark, for life!
Something like that, I think, was what he thought,
And the next morning, when the light grew up
In the open ports, on the ruin there—
The bottle and glasses, piles of clothes, that body
In stertorous sleep staining the white sheet—
He must have felt inside his mouth, on parts
Of body and soul he never knew he had,
A fungus only salt could eat away.
So he went topside, where sky and sea
And ship-at-work assembled his strewn parts
To Canot-in-command.
                              Ames was still drunk.
Burns had turned in, having had the deck till four
When Bouguereau relieved him. All night long
The HAPPY DELIVERY in a flat calm sea
And a quartering breeze had logged her seven knots.
The blacks below, from weariness and shock
Lay still all night, with only sounds of iron
And a desolate cry from sleep to speak their sorrow.

That morning Canot came to himself awake
When he caught that wraith of stink. It did not show
A picture of Recife, the great bark
Moving across his sight a growing stain:
Canot had no past, no yesterday.
The smell meant trouble, so he roused out Burns
To take the deck while he and Bouguereau
Made up a working party with armed guards
To bring the niggers up topside in shifts.
He broke out men to start the cooking fires
Under the try-pots. The blacks had to eat—
But if the breeze held and the sea stayed calm
They'd make Havana under fourteen days
With food to spare.
     They emptied the forward hold:
Niggers came topside, blinking, some of them fouled
With dung and urine. None had been seasick yet,
Thanks to the weather. The boatswain and his men
Herded them to the waist and forecastle
And gave them buckets and an old hand pump
And after they were clean, naked, and shivering
Under the climbing sun, each got a dipper
And scooped his meat and horsebeans from the try-pot.
Canot sent every man not working ship
Or busy with blacks down to the holds:
The stink was real there. The windsails had come down
To make more room topside. In those low spaces
Where Canot's cattle stalled, men stooped and squatted
With buckets, pumps, and hoses, sluicing down
The decks and bulkheads. After scrubbing clean
And clamping down, they sprinkled vinegar
And set a dozen tarpots smoldering
To clean the air. Canot had thought it out:
He'd take no chances. Keep the niggers fed,
The 'tween-deck clean and hope for strong fair winds:
The ship he could command. The wind was Chance's
Or Nature's or DaSouza's or Someone Else's—

Not his, he knew. But he would beat the world
Unless the world had heat to melt his ice,
Unfettle that steel brain. He drove the men.
He set a few to make the niggers dance—
Men and women both, and he stood by
To see the hands turned-to, no more than that,
No rutting season while he was in charge.
In the perfect air, between the vessel's elements
Of sea and sky, the blacks leaped to the drums
Or to the boatswain's cat, and sweat like grapes
Where sun struck through the droplets on black skin
Made Canot's flesh crawl, and he thought of *her*.
He sent the idle crewmen back below—
To fumigate, he said. He took no chances:
Let just one sailor leap a girl—no telling
What that would bring, but Canot made them fast
To duty till the niggers were played out.

The wind rose at sundown. Catspaw squalls
Wrinkling the surface came like sudden age,
And Burns, red-eyed from weariness, stared off
Ahead to the northwest where a loom of cloud
Was building from horizon to the zenith
In ochre, barbarous, unclean. He shook
His head and started aft. The vessel gave
A sodden lurch, throwing him off his feet,
As though the sea had parted, dropped away
And the ship had bottomed on a field of ice.
He picked himself up. Sounds from below
Frayed off in the steady breeze. The sails drew full
And the sea, dead-colored as a street at night,
Spread out ahead. Daylight plunged below
The curve of the world and Burns ran to the cabin scuttle
He found Ames in the half-lit master's cabin
Awake and sober, lying in his bunk
With bottles strewn and rolling on the deck.
"All empty, Burns," he said. "The best of 'em

Is here." He slapped his belly, belched, sat up
As Burns chased bottles gambolling like lambs
And tossed them out a port. "They'll mark our course.
You want a cruiser after us?" Burns came
To stand above him. "Weather's getting bad.
You get on deck where you belong to be."
"Where's Canot?" Ames stood up. Burns jerked his thumb
Pointing to Canot's cabin and Ames laughed.
"Maybe there's hope for us, then, hey? If Canot
Stays mounted on that bitch, maybe we'll work
This scow to Havana after all." Burns frowned
Hearing Ames call his ship a scow. He looked
More closely at him. "You too drunk to think?"
Ames laughed and slapped his shoulder. "It's all gone—
DaSouza's sherry and the owners' brandy.
From now on nigger rum—" A huge sideslip,
A shuddering falling away, as though a hand
Had pushed a crowd aside. Then a low moan
Distant, reverberant, in the air about them.
They looked at one another. "Rouse out Boats,"
Said Ames, and Burns ran full tilt to the ladder.
On deck, he felt at once his head had turned
And sent him to the hold, it seemed so close.
Under a cone of dark, a thin streak shone
Like candent steel where water touched the cloud .
The HAPPY DELIVERY stood up straight with sails
All luffed and sagging, while the helmsman spun
The great wheel and the ship's bow pointed west,
A broken gambler with his number up.
With quick sharp slaps like landed fish small waves
Splattered the hull, the water seemed to spurt
From pressure underneath in the windless air,
And Burns running forward thought he felt a strain
Under his feet, as though the sea grown huge
Was bursting irons and would cast this ship
In a vast expansion into outer dark.
The boatswain came to him with his pipe a-squeal

And men grew from the darkness to the shrouds
And skipped off out of sight among the tops
Or at the fore and mainmasts unbent halyards,
Hauled at the downhauls, taking canvas in.
Below a steady rumor, like the deep
And wordless anger of the lifting sea
Grew up and muted, grew again and steadied,
While over it the keener sounds of iron
And women's cries, the wailing of their young
Mingled with a twang like a plucked wire
That hummed and broke, as though the chain from heaven
To the world's cope parted at the touch of God.
Closed, as it seemed in glass, a model world
Containing echo, life, the hint of speed
Frozen forever in the builder's flask:
All hands, the ship and its unspeakable lade
Imperishably fixed. Then the sudden fall
Shattering to the chaos of the real.

VII.

Tropical storms, disturbances, typhoons:
You meet the smallest and you guess the largest:
Time gone out with light, and sea known now
For what it always was, a beast of prey.
Not fallen on Man: on You. Wet in the mouth
For blood of yours, a personal hate, unformed
And in a passionless frenzy cold to strike
The brain with madness, hot to try out heart
And spirit to despair, while flesh and bone—
Battered against the timbers of your world
Or swept deciduous to element—
Seem to run out like juice beneath a press.
Why try to tell a seaman things like this?
Biscay, the Caribbean, the Coral Sea,
Shoal water about Jutland, Hatteras,
Cape Esperance, New Georgia Sound, the Cuckolds,
The mouth of Fundy over Lurcher Shoal:

Terror by wind and water is the same
Yet private to each man, the enemy.
Each seaman has his storm special to him,
That separate searching-out by wind and water
That he remembers made him man and sailor;
And if remembering, he calls up pride
In muscle, skill, the suppleness to endure,
Let him remember better men hove-down,
Perhaps to spare him. Let him call it luck,
God's will, fate—anything but virtue.

There was a separate room in Canot's skull
Where he kept the gods he made and kept a flame
Alight forever on the knees of Chance,
Knowing that though he, Canot, knew himself
As free, no man's man, loose between ground and sky
With power to quell another with his will—
Knowing this much, he left in that cold head
A little place of fire where he worshipped
Alone, propitiating, vigilant to watch
How the flame might flicker and the Face might smile,
The smile of Chance, smiling to all; to some
Ironic, evil, to a Canot sweet,
For Chance is to the man who sees no evil.

It was so that day—that night—whatever time
May call itself when Nature bursts apart,
Ripping an arc from the universal sphere,
Seconds of time, moments of space blown up
To water, energy, the escape of mass.
At the second heave of the ship he'd come on deck
And seen the hands leap to the hurling spars
Before the rain exploded. Understand,
She had no way on, and the helm was down
And as the men aloft worked out along the footropes
And on deck a party fumbled at the sheets,
A wind as forced as air blown through hot steel

Fell on the deck. Her helm was down. The sails,
Not fully doused, blew up like paper bags.
The HAPPY DELIVERY, dragged by half of heaven,
Went down to her beam-ends in a rolling boil,
And as she skated forward on her side
The helm came up, weatherly, weatherly till
She snapped back upright and her masts sheared off
Clean at the goosenecks, and the deck planks gaped
Apart, she spat her oakum, spars and sails
Came down on deck athwartships, half inboard
Half spread to leeward, shrouding the dead and drowned.

Canot heard Bouguereau shout. The wind dropped flat
A moment, yet the pit of the storm cried out
Around them, echoing. Under their feet black flesh,
Resolving to its liquids, rolled in a flume
Like water falling to a power wheel:
No man's or woman's cry, no human fear,
The last leap of the blood gone back to slime.
Bouguereau, in that moment of roaring calm,
Broke free. He caught at Canot's arm: "The masts!
Clear the masts! We've got to clear the decks . . ."
He started toward the ladder from the poop
As the vessel fell away. When Canot looked
From thick cloacal dark, he saw him stride
On air—the sea split open like a berg
And the ship fetched up on rigid water
Starting her planks. The folding lip of a wave
Curled over her, warm and thickly salt as blood
Running away with ruin to the south;
High overhead a fever in the sky
Splattered strewn light. The rain rolled down again.
How long did it last? Time never stays to count.
The seas ran lower, the rain chased south, the sky
Broke up in patches. Canot looking forward
Could make out Bouguereau spraddled on a stump
Of mainmast. Then the dark closed in again.

Canot knew this much: no vessel built
Would live another hour lying slack
Untended. Letting rain press him to his knees
He slid across the deck and down the ladder,
And groping in the tangle found his way
To the mainmast-stump and Bouguereau. He shook
That body, clung as a sloth clings. "She'll go down!
Do something! Help me clear the masts and rigging . . ."
Bouguereau hugged his mast. A burst of wind
Struck water in their eyes and filled their mouths.
Canot tore at his shoulders, ripped him down
Sprawling on the deck, and he fell with him—
Both rolling there in the wash, till Canot pulled
Them both upright. "Go find me some men.
Get Burns and the boatswain. I'll find axes.
We'll get her through this yet." Bouguereau nodded.
"By God, you will," he said and started forward.
The wind still keened above them. Under his feet
Canot could feel the vessel sag and stagger
Like a rotten floor, though the seas were flattening out,
And below a scurry of torn greasy cloud,
Ocean ran sullen from its angry fit.
He slid athwartships to the boatswain's locker:
The lid was smashed but still inside were axes,
And splitting-knives. Rummaging, half-blind
With salt and water, he stood crouched and helpless
Till Bouguereau came with Burns, and the boatswain followed
Dragging a broken foot. In a long stillness,
They looked at each other, not quite sure of life,
And the vessel hung her head. They could not think
Of what the 'tween-deck held, though they heard it move
And grind in the foulness underneath their feet.
What men have done fades out in what's to do.
In an instant's pause, while rain boomed dense as surf,
Canot had scrambled to the waist with Burns,
The boatswain, and Bouguereau. It was still.
Wind roared out of the darkness overhead

In a sound of caissons rolling to a war
While water like an ocean overturned
Caught at the knives and axes until Canot
In a wide arc struck the lopped stump of the mainmast
And the parted shrouds, the jungle of hemp, wood, cloth
Carried the rail away and disappeared.
They cleared the foremast tangle then. Chance smiled
And Canot, always watchful, saw the smile.
The ship, in stillness, for the rain had lessened,
Like a forest lumbered out, lay piled with slash—
Mutilate, sodden, as the sea ran in
Her open seams. The men looked at each other—
Canot and Burns, the boatswain and Bouguereau—
Then aft where Ames stood, spread against the wheel,
While out of silence, all the 'tween-decks roared.
Above, white-hot distemper tattered the dark.
The sea below, like writhing oil, in spurts
Flickered darts of spray straight up and the wind
Rolled southward. "Turn the niggers up," said Canot.
Burns looked at him. "Turn up hell," he said.
"We'll turn them up and pump her out. Here, Bouguereau,
You come with me."
                        The mainhatch cover was sprung
But they forced it with an axe. I leave to you
What lifted up that lid. What plumps the skin
Of bodies ten days drowned? Fat as a grease,
A sewer-rime asweat where sunlight strikes,
The uncabined genie blundered on the air
And Canot, with his leg athwart the coaming,
Fell back on Bouguereau. Spirit of that stench,
The noise boiled with it, thick and low as rot.
Bound hordes there tumbling in a roll of filth—
Sphincters and bellies of mankind all loose,
And Canot would go down to turn that up!
As though gone back to its original slime,
Wallowing, powerless to rise or crawl,
The fit of Adam's flesh undone, the journey

98

From dark to light turned back: what was down there
Belonged to Canot, belonged to all of them.
Still sea, a hurrying of cloud above the sea,
A hull that welcomed water, pointing home
With downcast head. The crew was torn in half
By the stripping of the rigging, and the rest
Had huddled near the hatch. Ames, at the wheel,
Clung to the spokes as though spread on a rack,
Stunned, motionless. The wild noise from the hold
Had dimmed to animal rumor, beyond fear,
Pulsing like breath, a quivering exhalation,
While over the deck in an unshifting pall
The effluent-laden air took fungoid shape
Commingling seminal and graveyard breaths.

Canot bound a wet rag over his face,
The others watched him. He still had the axe:
Holding it edge-first, to cut the air
It seemed, he grasped the handhold and went down
And Bouguereau blew his breath out in a hiss.
No sound—only the quivering stricken breath
And the spring noise of water at the seams.
"Better abandon," Burns said, looking away,
And Bouguereau laughed: "Abandon? Into what?"
The deck was clean—longboat, dingies gone
With pennants of hemp where the slings had held them fast.
It struck home then: hurt to death, perhaps,
Drinking the ocean and settling down to sleep
The HAPPY DELIVERY lifted to a swell
Undulant, barely rising. Then a sound
Repeated, hard, the axe firm to its work
And a hubbub of voices with Canot's voice above it.
"Abandon! Here, stand back," and Bouguereau
Had plunged to the ladder and gone out of sight
While the others stood there. Burns had turned away.
He shook himself. "Open the forward hatch,"
He said, not really thinking what he said,

And they went forward—sailors once again.
The vessel lifted again, gently, living.
"We'll pump her out, by God," Burns said. "She'll live
And get us home yet."
                                        All that night they worked.
They roused the blacks out, took their irons off
And set them to the pumps. Burns formed a line
From hold to bulwarks, passing corpses up,
And by dawn the holds were clear and the water-level
Below their ankles. Now her head was high
And she rode like a gull, swinging to face the wind
And yearning for her sails. By noon the sun
Had dried and warmed her, though the wraiths of steam
Came up like rotten breath from carious mouths.
The blacks lay all about, leached white it seemed,
Like litter left above high-water mark.
Canot had fires made and food sent round
And some of them ate, looking off to windward
While over the leeward side the bodies splashed
Dark there an instant till a slash of fins,
A rending sound, a thrash of overthrow,
Then a red widening stain: the sharks were fed.
By sunset they had jury-rigged the ship
With spars made fast to the stumps of fore and mainmasts
And with a fresh breeze just abaft the beam
The HAPPY DELIVERY, on her middle passage
And riding high and light, clipped to the westward.
Two hundred blacks were rolling in her wake;
A dozen seamen, casuals of storm,
Had furled in canvas to a sudden end;
The vessel's master, dosed by Canot's drugs,
Lay in his bunk till he should wake to madness,
And Canot drove them all, men, slaves, and ship,
Until night fell and every man on board
Dropped where he stood—except for Bouguereau
And Canot who had still their ship to work,
A cargo to deliver, and their youth.

For Canot was young that night. He had not slept
Nor rested since the night before, and standing
Aft near the wheel and looking to the west
Where the ash of sun still burned he felt a pride:
Bouguereau had followed. He had led.
The vessel, crew and cargo were all his
By right of fortitude. The wheel groaned once
As Bouguereau kept course, and Canot thought
Of her, below, locked in. He turned and nodded
To Bouguereau: "I'll be right back," he said
And went below. He paused by Ames's cabin
Listening a moment to the broken sounds
Of madness drugged. He found his cabin key
And went inside. There was glass strewn on the deck,
But nothing else. She lay in the bunk asleep
And Canot took her as she lay, cold, still:
She might have been a corpse. He did not care.
When he had finished, he poured out some rum
Into a tumbler and drank it off, then handed
The bottle to the girl. She lay there still,
The wide eyes fixed. Her hand closed round the bottle
And Canot laughed: "You know what's good for you,"
Watching as she tilted it and drank
And darkness flooded her eyes. He turned and left her.
Outside the cabin door the passageway
Felt close. The open scuttle framed the night
Above his head, a well cast upside down,
And as he climbed the ladder, going deeper
Into the headlong midwatch of the voyage,
He seemed closed in by tunnel walls, water
And darkness, while about him unseen eyes
Followed his movement, he himself alone
And lost. Then, feet loud on the deck,
A single star to the west and a loom of sail,
The world swam upright. He saw Bouguereau
Spread to the wheel like Ixion, like a slave
A god has bound to keep the world still turning.

He stood beside him. "Get below," he said
And handed him the cabin key. "Two hours.
Relieve me here at four. Don't fall asleep."
"No fear," said Bouguereau, and looked aloft a moment
At the western star. "That should be Aldebaran."
He turned toward the scuttle ladder. "Funny thing—
Storms and work and danger make me sharp."
Canot, with his back turned, turned the wheel
And Bouguereau went down, under the star.

VIII.

Those three nights underway from Baltimore
Bowling along before a southwest breeze
I lived an age—my own youth, Canot's odyssey,
And something of America's rise and fall.
Don't ask why I say "fall." *You'd* call it change
Or progress or a frontier opening up—
Some sentimental ice-cream words, like calling
Death by another name. But death won't change
Though you may, with your head in sands of lies.
It gets in your mouth, eyes, and ears. Or if not yours
Somebody else's—never yours and mine—
Those famous others who never see the real . . .
I saw it then, with Canot for a glass.
I was sixty-five and I left the sea that fall
To settle here in Salem, just like Canot,
Though not in Salem earth. At least not yet.
That bark was my last command, my last sea voyage . . .
Nowadays, in spring when the weather's fair,
I walk to the Willows and look off
Past Misery Island, thinking of not much
Or far too much. I've been to Canot's grave—
Put flowers on it too! How he'd have laughed!
And so do you—and I did at the time—
My sentimental ice-cream irony.
Yes, he would have laughed. Broke, dying, sick
With pain, and sleepless, nothing touched his will.

I asked him once, the last night out. We'd gone
Topside—the first time Canot'd left the cabin
And the night was moonless, star-coined, soft to touch.
We sat on some after bitts, our backs against
The taffrail, and Canot listened to the night
And I wondered, wondered what swam in that head
Up from the images foundered years and fathoms
Below the surface. "Do you have regrets?'
I asked him. "That is, for your life—the past
And all you did—both of us? All that . . ."
I wondered. I confess I was afraid—
Afraid that Canot, dead as my own youth,
Had learned to fear, grown old, become a child
Afraid of the Good Bogey in the sky
And the Bad Bogey in the cellar. So I stammered
And Canot fixed me with that stringent eye
While the nose twitched like a dog's. "I went too far—
Farther than you. And may have seen things there—
There at the bottom. The world is upside down:
I found that out, and going down, went up.
While *you*—" he twitched his nose and cocked a glance—
"You hoisted down. The moral man." Just then
The boatswain on his rounds came up. "Beg pardon, Cap'n.
I heard a voice . . ." "It's all right, Boats," I said
And he looked at Canot and went on up forward.
"I've no regrets!" The tone was hard but low:
"No after-praying, deathbed mercy-on-me's
For what a man does that others want
But will not do, for fear of botch—afraid
To see the muck their fortunes breed and die in.
I'd do it all again—" He turned on me
With the light-gathering eyes and foreign slant
To nose and lips, as if the tallying angel
Were checking all the facts against his story.
"What do you know, you sailors?" "Nothing much,
And that's the truth," I said, half to myself,
While Canot laughed. "Oh you're an honest man,

I'll ask *you* to regret—for both of us."
He stopped there. Then, as though he'd found the page
Where he'd left off, he started on his tale,
His voice a pulsebeat of the summer night,
The unhurried speed of stars away from earth.

Dawn broke. The overcast threw splintered cloud
Across the sky, and the tradewind pushed them on,
While day grew up in heavy sunlight lain
Along the deck. It soaked down to the hold
And though the crew rigged windsails at each hatch,
Though Canot brought the blacks topside for air,
Filth seeped out sinking into uncaulked seams
And plumped up sails distending like drowned bellies.
They pumped. God, how they pumped. All day in shifts
The black and white men sweated there together
Below decks with the slime of vomit, dung
And urine under foot, while out on deck
The women and children lay like broken dolls
Quiet except for coughing. That first day
After the storm Canot had cut their rations,
For half their stores had spoiled in brine in the forepeak
And there were days and days until Havana.
Late that afternoon when the heat was less
And the breeze grew fresh, Bouguereau went below
And knocked at Canot's cabin door. By this time
Canot was spending all his hours off duty
There with the girl. Once or twice a day
He gaves Ames laudanum in a tot of rum
And left him there to rave back into sleep.
Between times, Bouguereau kept Canot's key
And made himself at home. They slept a little
Between bouts with the girl. They kept her moving!
This was the night each of them went at her
Successively while the other stayed to watch,
And for the first time Canot used his drugs
On her and them. They let Burns keep the deck

104

All night, though at the first watch Canot went
Topside to relieve him, offering the girl
And all the amenities, but Burns declined—
Not shocked, apparently; just not interested.
Later Bouguereau, at the forenoon watch,
Came up to relieve but Canot sent him down
To check the carpenter's work caulking the seams.
He came back quickly: there were several dead
And a dozen or so coughing out their guts.
They roused them all out, crowded in the waist
And as they came out over the high coamings
A number tripped and stumbled. A few lay
Where they had fallen. Lashes did no good.
Canot went down from the poop. The wind still blew
Fair from the sou'west. Even with that rig
The HAPPY DELIVERY was logging her six knots
And Canot knew they'd make it to Havana.
Yet would the cargo spoil? He looked at them:
The women were mostly silent now. The children,
All under ten or so, were in the wake
And bait for sharks. Well, they had little value.
But the men: at the mainhatch Canot saw them lying
Staring into the sky. His heart pulsed heavily,
For some were blind. He looked down at a face
Peakéd and sunk, the deadlights of the eyes
Were blacked-out ports. The pink voluted ears
Wide-angled from the head had never heard him
Nor the tongue, thick as a hawser, given him speech.
Canot put out his hand to hold the jaw
And look more closely but then jerked it back
Glancing about. The others, blacks and seamen
Withdrawn in loneliness, sickness, fear or hunger
Cared nothing. He drew his hand across his eyes
And went back aft. "Ophthalmia," he said
And Bouguereau made a face. "Jesus, I knew it!
I've heard of it before—" "Well, now we've got it
Or most of us will." They looked down to the waist:

The carpenter came up the mainhatch ladder
Rubbing his eyes. "Christ," said Bouguereau
And Canot clamped his wrist. "Get him below—
To Ames's cabin. I'll see what I can do.
We can't let him go blind . . ." "What about Burns?"
Bouguereau looked forward where Burns stood
In exhausted stoop, lashing some fallen blacks.
"You and I can't navigate. If he . . ."
Canot pushed him away. "Get Chips down there!
Ames has Bowditch, another Salem boy,
And if I have to learn how to catch stars,
I'll learn." "In a day?" "In a day! Why not? You keep
This thing afloat. I'll get it to Havana."

        Canot might have wondered how his eyes
Would see beyond disease, catch stars, dead reckon
And unsnarl the knots of logarithmic tables.
He might have, but he didn't, knowing his luck
Like a blind man's dog would lead him past abysses
To trust in luck, to back it up with work
And let the future happen. As he gazed
From the poop down to the litter on the deck—
The bodies strewn, the waste of a stricken field—
He rummaged back in his mind for remedies
And palliatives remembered from the days
Of Smith's apothecary shop
When March came in with bronchial catarrhs,
Cat fever, pinkeye—that was what it was,
Pinkeye! All that filth, the close-packed decks
Had bred ophthalmia. Now to remember
The eyewash, the drug, the balm to bathe the infection.
He saw the carpenter, led by Bouguereau,
Move aft below him. He could bathe their eyes
As many as he could with what he had.
After that—well, the sea air and clean sunlight
Would do the trick—if things weren't gone too far.

Burns took the deck. Canot went below.
He'd win. He'd beat them yet—Bliss, Crane and Salem,
Sea and the plague. He felt as strong as God.

The afternoon lay heavy on the ship
Yet she bore on bravely under her clumsy rig
And with her patched-up seams. The pumps were still
Most of the time now, and both crew and blacks
Huddling in shade, waited for death or Cuba
As strength oozed out. They'd had their single meal
At noon—spoiled beef, some beans, a pan of water.
There would be nothing more, by Canot's order,
Till noon next day. They lay or sat or leaned
Waiting for blindness. Canot went his round
Among the whites and swabbed the red-rimmed eyes,
Talking, talking, telling them not to fear,
The darkness would pass over, that he'd seen
This blindness come and go again. They sat
And let him pour his unguents. Minute by minute
As the sun in easy fall, in hours of time,
Degrees of arc and distance, moved toward night
They bore to the westward. Men lay where they were
And no one moved but the helmsman to his wheel,
Waiting for the darkness. Burns was there
Asleep under the poopdeck overhang
As though no more could happen. Canot unlocked
The door of Ames's cabin and went in.
The old man lay there, his white sunken face
Like a dirty rag on the pillow and he looked
With living eyes at Canot. The old madness
And drugged despair had drained away and left
Something of the man.
                          "You having trouble?"
Ames's voice was thin but it was his
Again, a little rusty from exposure
And neglect. As Canot filled a glass

With rum and laudanum, Ames swung from the bunk
And grasped a chair back, hauling himself erect.
"No thanks, sawbones. I'll leave that alone.
I'm in command now . . ."
                    Canot held the tumbler
Halfway between them.
                        "Drink it down," he said.
"I've seen it through without your help till now.
Lie down. You're dead. Dead and almost buried."
Ames looked at him. From next door they heard
A whistling sigh, the creak of wood, a burst of speech
High in an unknown tongue.
                        "You shared your whore
With Bouguereau. You'll share a rope together
When we get home . . ." Canot laughed at him,
That neighing laugh through the nose we both remember
And Ames shrank back, though upright still. "I warn you
It's mutiny—and worse . . ."
                        Canot came forward
And placing his palm quite gently on his chest,
Pushed once. The feeble, ravaged body fell
Against the bunk, collapsed.
                        "You'll hang—" His eyes
Wide and drugged with terror. "I'll stay here,
Let me alone . . ." The body crumpled up
And Canot held the pillow to the face,
His own head up and facing toward the stern
Where through a port a risen planet pulsed,
And watching so he felt the life go out
Beneath his hands, while from the other cabin
In rutting tremor, Bouguereau and the girl
Played out their game.
                        He lifted up the pillow
And without looking seized the hair and slipped
The pillow under the head. It had no weight
It seemed. He turned, went out, and locked the door.

IX.

On that last morning, northeast from Baltimore,
Canot came on deck as we stood in
And sat by the taffrail watching the harbor tug
Take hold and warp us into the Mystic basin
And up against the pier. Our lines went over,
The sails came down, and I was there alone,
Except for Canot, with my last command,
All ocean and my life behind my back
And ahead of me a few years till the grave.
You'd think, in such a moment, time would spin
The past before your eyes, taking its leave,
But there was nothing: only foul water,
The warehouse roofs, a glimpse of human life
In houses up the hill, a sunlit steeple.
The sea behind, hid by the river's curve,
Had done with me and cast me up to dry.
It was then I noticed Canot, who had come
To the gangway. For an instant we were there
Together, of an age, a height, a figure
And dressed alike, for Canot wore the clothes
I'd given him to fit him for his grave.
He looked at me and smiled. I looked away.
"What about money?" "I've enough," he said.
"The Merchants Bank will stake me to a coffin
And there's the family lot back of the church—
Unless they keep me out . . ."
                                        "Why? Who's to say
You can't have Christian burial?" "Oh, Christians,
And Salem. Salem's the Hebrew word for peace . . ."
I looked at him. "I can't go with you now,"
I said. "I've work to do unloading cargo
And seeing the owners . . ." "Never mind. I'll make
My own return. You've troubles of your own.
You'll have to live there and I wouldn't help you."

He stood on the gangplank, empty-handed, thin,
Unlike me as a shadow, moved apart,
With water foul below him and on shore
New England soil—cobbles, brick and ash.
I heard the mate's voice calling, and I turned;
Before I could look back, Canot was gone
Among the sheds, the factories, stockades
Of junkyards, slaughterhouses, tenements
With fifteen miles between him and his grave.
How did I know that—know his death so near?
He said so, and I never doubted Canot,
Who never lied, nor needed to, being sure
None would believe his truth unless they knew him.
And I had known him. It was time to die
And take the secret underground. He knew
I could not last forever, and what harm
To tell me, give himself away to me—
A broken sailor, whom the sea spewed out?
And so I tell you, now, believing Canot
Wherever he has gone, will have his laugh
At you and me disturbing his dried bones,
His special horror. Can you hear him laugh?
We shrank from him in life. In death he owns us,
Friends of his bosom, comrades, sons in evil,
We who simply lived while Canot died—he must have
Night after night on that first middle passage,
Died out of youth, out of innocence, romance
And—it may sound foolish, out of the real—
Died into Power, into Canot pure.

On deck night lay, a bandage layer on layer
Impenetrable by air or healing touch:
The vessel in surreptitious passage groaned,
The steering cables murmured on their sheaves,
Dark of the moon. Canot walked that deck
Past clumps of bodies, dying, blind alive,

Asleep or drowned by fear. What could he do,
One man alone? When Bouguereau came up
To take the deck, Canot did not leave
But stayed far forward in the chains with eyes
Devouring miles of sea and night. When dawn
With whispers of new air and level silver
Over the eastern sill would speak of hope,
Only the hull, the canvas moving her,
Felt other than despair. The night drained off
As the world tilted. Canot saw it spill
And as he waited for the sea to turn,
A hull loomed from the mist broad on the bow,
Hove-to, her rigging slack and dripping damp.
On the windward ratlines one man stood alone
And waved. His voice came faint as a wraith of fog:
"Position! Give us position! We are blind.
All hands are blind. Please. Tell us where we are . . ."
The mist divided them. The HAPPY DELIVERY
Slid sighing into fog, the voice choked off
And Canot had for memory that vision:
A black hull riding out of mist, one man,
His single voice as piping as a tern's,
A mirror and an echo! Was this all?
This was the end? A death by salt and dark?
Where were they? Bound to circles of the sphere
And doomed to sail on, rotting one by one
Fettered to one another and the sea?
He jumped to the forecastle. In the foggy dawn
He saw Burns next a pile of capstan bars
Asleep or dead, his wide beard on his breast,
And Canot stirred him with his foot.
                                        "Get up!"
Burns moved and groaned. Canot bent down
And hauled him to his feet, propping his back
Against the foremast. Burns's eyes were red
And gummed like sores. He laid his arm across them.

"Let me alone, you devil. Let me die,
Go back to sleep and die . . ." A few men stirred
Hearing that voice: "Heave the bastard over . . ."
But Canot heard another voice, that echo,
And saw that mirror only. They both lied!
Now let Chance speak! Let Luck find its voice:
For a moment he stood, his right hand pinning Burns
By the shoulder to the mast while the left had grasped
The breast of Burns's shirt and rags of beard,
As Canot's voice—he knew it must be Canot's—
Spilled curses, filth, as though he were below
Riding that girl and pumping out himself.
Under his hands Burns quivered. Let Chance speak.
Mist parted, sun in a shaft as hard as ice
Broke through and shattered color on the deck.
A sign? Who knows? The sun was low astern
And the HAPPY DELIVERY ran on in her groove,
The middle passage paved by thousands drowned.

That day, while Bouguereau stood to the wheel
And Canot cleared corpses from the deck,
The wind held fair and steady, driving them on.
All day the white men swabbed their eyes with salves
And Canot tended Burns and made him eat
Until, at evening twilight, Burns could stand
Beside him. When the stars showed, Canot took
Some sights by quadrant while Burns held the watch
And coached him pulling stars down. Canot took
A dozen sights and made Burns, step by step,
Take him through the tables, and at last
By midnight they were fixed upon the chart,
A tiny triangle whence they must take departure.
The taffrail log, still streaming in their wake,
Made certain they were doing their five knots.
And Canot set his pencil down. Three days
At least before a landfall—with fair winds.
Nature conspired, and the trade wind blew:

Now to keep life alive, to bring back sight
And clear the Windward Islands before dawn.

Oh, he was a favorite son that time, that voyage.
He knew it, and he backed the favorite
With all his capital of youth, brains, strength, and skill
To pull light out of dark, stars out of space,
And fix the HAPPY DELIVERY on her course
With Bouguereau to help. No trips below
For them now. If they ever thought of her—
And Canot must have—it would have been in hate
At least with Canot.
                              Bouguereau would shrug
Inside himself and laugh at certain memories.
Well, what about her, after all? The night
Before they entered harbor, Canot went
Below to Ames's cabin. It was foul
And close. He spread the stern ports wide.
They were broad as windows, trimmed outboard with gilt
And shapes of shutters painted on the stern.
He dragged the stinking body, wrapped in blankets,
Up on the transom seat and bent it back
With head and shoulders leaning out the ports,
It poised a moment there. The blankets lapped
Away from the head and the sunken yellow face
Looked up to the sky, Deneb, Aldebaran,
The usable sailor's heaven. Canot heaved
At the legs, the slack waist sagged, the trunk edged out
Across the sill and Canot heaved again.
The upper body dropped and the legs flew up
Striking Canot sidelong on the head;
A foot caught in the corner port
A moment. Canot tore at it and the body—
Spread-eagled and slack—slumped down against the rudder.
Then after huddling there an instant, lapsed
To the quiet wake and rolled back into night.
Canot sat down trembling. He was weak

From sleeplessness. A creaking of a hinge
Made him look up. Bouguereau stood there
In the doorway.
        "Burns can see a bit. I set him
To mind the helm—" He stopped and looked about.
A curtain trembled, then drew out the port
And Bouguereau smiled. "Congratulations, captain . . ."
He said as Canot rose, like an old man.
"So Ames got the deep six . . ."
        "He was dead," said Canot
And leaned on the table lest he shake to pieces.
"Dead—or killed? Who cares? Who knows, in fact?"
"You do," said Canot, lifting his heavy eyes.
But Bouguereau looked out the port. "I know.
I was next door." "But busy," Canot said.
Bouguereau smiled again: "She lost a lot
After that storm. The girl's not worth the effort . . ."
"We'll be in port tomorrow afternoon";
Canot straightened up. He did not tremble.
"What will you say?" The other did not smile
This time. "You got us through. I don't care how
You did it. As for Ames—I'd be back there"—
He nodded aft—"A couple hundred miles . . .
I'll keep my mouth shut." Canot blew a breath
From between his teeth. Bouguereau went on:
"We'd better fix that girl. She knows a lot."
"What can she say?" Canot ground it out.
"Enough. She knows some English, didn't you know?"
Canot put out a hand, then pulled it back
As though he'd touched a flame. "I don't believe it . . ."
"Why not? DaSouza had her first. She wasn't
A virgin when you had her at his house.
He taught her some. She told me so. At first
She kept her mouth shut—she was afraid of you."
"I'll see to her." Canot went toward the door
But Bouguereau took his arm. "There's no use killing her.
She'll die by morning anyhow, with no food

Or water for a few days. Only rum . . ."
But Canot had wrenched free and gone outside.
He unlocked the door, went in and closed and locked
Himself in there—with her. She lay stark naked
In the bunk, her eyes like coalholes, without source
Or light beneath. Her breathing, bubbling out
Between her teeth, filled up the room with noise
And Canot saw her body had gone gray
And thinly slack. He'd browsed across that field.
Only the welts, the manual of his hate,
Sprang to his eyes: the coinlike rosy burns
Inside her thighs, the cracked scab at her breast,
And Canot's stomach rose; he could not stop it
But vomited sourly on the cabin floor.
Her breathing stopped, rattled, struggling out
As though the life like a bird beat against mesh.
He turned to the door, the vomit on his shoes
Followed him to the ladder and the deck
Where he bent, untied them, threw them over the side.
After that he lay down next a hawser
And slept till dawn, dreamless and without stir,
While in the west the islands, teemed with life,
Grew up in darkness with no emanation
Of scent or bird or traffic reaching out
To touch the HAPPY DELIVERY.
                              The next morning
The crew was mustered aft. They numbered twelve.
Some ten could see again, a few could work
And Burns had driven them to make anchors ready.
Now all was done. Ahead the purple mass
Of Cuba leaned on water, green and white,
Before it fathomed deeper into blue,
And off to starboard, crowding under sail
Set high and full, vessels bore east or north
And left them single, running in a groove.
Canot stood at the fife rail, Bouguereau
A pace behind him. Burns was at the helm

And the crew, all twelve of them, around the mainmast
Erect or sitting, heard his thin voice move
Weightlessly over them.
                                    "I've counted up
Some eighty blacks who'll fetch the market price.
The rest—there should be only ten or so—
We'll take what we can get for them . . . Your shares
Will be according to our first agreement.
Mr. Burns and Mr. Bouguereau
Will have the mates' shares. The captain's goes to me . . ."
I doubt if they heard him, any of them.
At any rate, when Canot gave the word
To rouse the blacks out, not a man moved.
He said it again. No answer, no response.
Burns at the helm gazed forward toward the land
Mounting in separate colors, shapes and features—
A place, an island, and an end. Then Canot
Reached back: "Your pistol, Mr. Bouguereau."
He felt the barrel cold within his palm.
"Turn to," he said. The boatswain spat on deck,
And Canot shot him. The unrifled bore
Puffed smoke, the boatswain tumbled to his knees
With blood wetting his trousers from inside
And Canot nearly laughed. Just like a child
Caught short. The others scrambled to their feet
And Canot gave the pistol back to Bouguereau.
"See they rouse those niggers out, Mr. Burns,"
He said, and sent a seaman to the wheel.

They ate and drank the last of their supplies,
Those who could eat or drink. The vessel held
A point or two on the wind to clear the cape
And land was very near. They entered harbor
At six, running before the breeze to anchorage.
Burns had taken bearings on the shore
And the anchor dropped at half-past six in ten
Fathoms of water, with an ample scope of cable,

The sails were doused and lay bunched on the deck
And men lay on them, their middle passage done.
The agent's longboat came up alongside
And Canot asked for a lighter to unload
The blacks before he'd leave his first command.
    By nine that evening, all hands were ashore:
Slaves at the market, crew in hospital
Except for the hardier souls in whorehouse beds.
And Canot, with his first mate Bouguereau,
Both of them clean and fitted with new clothes,
Sat with the agent at a café table.
The HAPPY DELIVERY, resting on her chain
In charge of a shipkeeper and a mongrel dog,
Was out of Canot's sight and mind. Oh yes:
I've told you Canot had no past, no yesterdays.
He was no seaman, either, and his ship
Could rot there, now he'd brought her where it paid.
Sitting there, Bouguereau, who was no Canot
Whatever else he was, watched those two strangers
Drinking Parisian absinthe. Did he wonder
How he had got there? Something of the sort
I think. He left the trade for Navy life
And that's a jump—for sailors, anyhow.
The agent was largesse itself—free liquor,
A dinner that DaSouza might have envied,
A little ready cash. What more would you
Or I have wanted, on a summer night
In Havana, at nineteen, after a passage?
The agent—a smooth gentleman with rings
Knuckle to knuckle across small white hands—
Let Bouguereau drink up while he spread papers
And talked to Canot—and let Canot talk.
At length the agent rose.
                          "The bill is mine,
As was the pleasure, gentlemen.—No, please.
Another engagement. Mr. Bouguereau,
I have enjoyed this meeting. Yes, at ten,

Mr. Canot.—Do enjoy yourselves—"
And he was gone. The café had grown full;
One or two women, sliding past, had paused
But Canot did not look, and Bouguereau
Was waiting.
             "Well, what now? Do we get paid
Tomorrow?" Canot looked askance at him.
"I'm selling him the lot. You're free to go
Tomorrow when I get the cash." He paused:
"You know, we were overdue. Another ship
Reported us as lost after that storm . . ."
Bouguereau tried to meet those sidelong eyes
But Canot was filling his glass and needed them:
"Bliss and Crane have filed for the insurance
So I figured that the vessel must be mine.
He wanted to buy me out . . ."
                 Bouguereau grinned:
"Buy your tongue, you mean! He'll get the ship,
Rename her and all he needs is a little quiet
From you . . ."
         "And you, too," Canot said. He finished
His glass of cognac. "There's a Spanish bark
In port—she's fitting for a slaving voyage
And needs a master. I thought you and I
Might try again—we won't have bad luck twice,
Not if I know." The other looked at him:
"You'd go straight back there—now?"
               Canot looked down
And cupped the glass in his prehensile hand:
"I'll never go back home. I've gone too far.
You're Southern—you don't know. Once a New Englander
Heads out and away, there's no end to his travels . . ."
It was the first time Canot had dropped guard
And mask together. Looking up, he saw
His shipmate, bluff Ned Bouguereau, a blond
Wide-faced and open animal, taking in
What he could take of Canot thus revealed

118

And Canot hardened. I can see those eyes
Grow dense, refractive, icy, shedding light
As Bouguereau, with something close to friendship,
Reached out.
            The mask dropped down—perfect disguise
To make you feel you'd followed a mirage.
"There's thousands to be made. This barque's got space
For fifteen hundred blacks. She's big and roomy
But plenty fast—or so the agent said.
I thought you and I could look at her tomorrow . . ."
The café was full now but a cone of silence
Was over them. A tan girl in bright silk
Came weaving fore and aft up to their table
But must have noticed something—those girls have to—
And did not stay. Bouguereau looked down
At his hands, thick, knotty brown on the white marble,
A sailor's hands, you'd say—good for all jobs.
He wagged his head. "I guess not, Mr. Canot;
I want a change. Slaving's not my trade . . ."
Canot rasped back his chair. He never argued
Or wasted anything. "Too bad," he said.
"I might as well try Burns . . ." The other stared,
Half-disappointed he had not been urged:
"Burns? Burns is at the bitter end, I'd say . . ."
"Perhaps. Perhaps not. He's from New England, too."
And Canot rose at that.
                    "Be at the office
At ten tomorrow and I'll pay you off . . ."
"You staying on the ship? That girl's still there
If I remember rightly . . ."
                    Canot smiled.
"You don't remember rightly, Mr. Bouguereau.
In fact, if I were you, I'd not remember
A single person I could put a name to—
Not even a place. Pretend it never happened.
To ease your conscience—or just to stay alive.
Ten tomorrow, then."

He left at that.
It might have pleased him had he stayed to see
If Bouguereau were afraid. I'm sure he was.
I would have been. Oh, not of threats of violence
But just of Canot. Canot was a force
Worked free of nature but with nature's power
Become his own by separate mastery—
By such perverse destruction of himself
As makes a mystic or a saint but anyhow
Makes power. Bouguereau was hard enough
But seamanlike and innocent. He knew
The place for him was out of this. He finished
His brandy at a gulp and went outside
Into the tangible Caribbean night
And Canot, waiting in a darkened doorway,
Saw him take up with the first girl to come his way,
And you and I can understand: the touch
Of human love, crude, cash-on-the-barrelhead
Must have been what he needed. Canot watched
The two fade down the street and put away
His notion. Why kill Bouguereau? He saw
The boy for what he was: a simple sailor
Who'd talk and talk, perhaps, mixing up lies
With truth till he believed it all alone.
Bouguereau was safe. No one would bother.
He went back for the last time to his vessel
In a harbor wherry and told the man to wait.
The shipkeeper, dozing by the Jacob's ladder,
Said nothing. His mongrel yawned and cocked an eye,
Then stretched his muzzle on the deck, and Canot
Went down to the cabin and unlocked the door.
He stood a moment in the airless hush
And felt under his feet the vaguest lift
Of ocean, tide swift-running from the moon,
As though drowned supplicant hands reached for the hull.
He waited there, nothing behind his eyes
To see, to curse him, or to touch his senses,

About him timber, planking, smooth and snug
In join and angle as a coffin. Silence,
An unlocked presence behind unlocked doors,
Awaited him. Canot was not afraid:
The girl was dead. Who on earth or Cuba
Would ask a question for a dead black girl?
Then why did he go back there, knowing that,
And fearing nothing, with no cause to fear?
He went back to his vomit, like a dog!
Inside, a wasted light came through the port
From the lantern on the poop above his head.
She lay in a wash of amber that filled out
Her scoops and hollows and starved eyes with shadow,
More kind than light. The scars at breast and thighs
Were hid below that shroud, the laying-out
The ship alone had worked. Canot looked down
And hatred welled up. Did he see her there
By fire on her side, one leg drawn up
And turning, taking him into herself alive?
I tell you, he saw nothing—nothing—ever.
He felt a hate as abstract as a line
Starting from nothing, ending nowhere, ever.
DaSouza by the window, rainy sounds
Of wind in palms, the bed enmeshed and dim,
His first love, seeded fruitless in that womb . . .
Standing there, his hands hung at his sides
And working, as though trying to work free
To reach in love, Canot was still,
His mask in perfect place, never to lift
Until a brief span before his death,
He let me see below. Nothing was there.
The mask had worn the features to a plane
Abstract, indifferent, fearful to God alone.
And upright on his bones disguised with flesh
Canot let hands and fingers search the table
To find a bottle. The left hand took it up
By the neck, and with a perfect strike

On the brassbound table-edge, cracked off the base
Leaving a saw-toothed truncheon in the fist.
It raised, came down over the ruined face,
Ground in a circle with the body's weight
Behind it. Then released.
                    Canot went out.
The door was open, swaying in the draft,
Forever clicking at the latch and banging
Softly against the stop as the vessel surged.

It's late. Look how the moon has sought the West.
Looking across the bay, if we could see it,
The east would ooze at the edges with a flood
Of dawn and the old circle full again.
We're old, both of us. The sea's behind us
Whether we look at it or turn our backs
And we'll be ashes others may rake over,
As we have done tonight with Canot's leavings.
Strange, I keep on saying that I'm old
But I don't *feel* old, always—not even much
Of the time, especially now that spring is here
With geese overhead and alewives in the creeks.
I look about more since I left off seagoing
And settled for a mansion and a housekeeper.
I even feed the birds! Aye, that's old age,
To value the cheapest life—even your own.
You'll come to it.
                    Tomorrow afternoon
(Today, rather; I don't keep track of time
Since all my navigation now's dead reckoning)
We'll go to the churchyard and see Canot's grave—
Oh yes, they let him in! I told them to
If they cared to be legatees under my will.
They think I'm filthy rich—and they're quite right,
But it doesn't do, in Salem, to show it off,
Except for buying people. That makes Salem
A cut above the others, who play games

With money, and the people think they're free.
New Englanders know everything costs cash,
That every sale is profit for one party
And ruin for the other. Calvinism
Is what they used to call it. Now the Irish
Have changed the names but it's the same hard bargain
—You're right. It's late. Too late to get on that,
To finger your own wen, with pain and pleasure;
But it's built into us. We'll do it still
When Maine's a summer brothel to Chicago.
This afternoon then. Kindly omit flowers;
I won't have Canot laughing from his grave!
You know these steps—the gate's by McIntire
In case you care. Restored, or so they tell me,
Which may be more than you and I will be.
Goodnight—good morning, rather. Which way's east?
Oh yes, I forget with all these landmarks here
That never move but set where they arose.
There's one star left—up there above the elm—
Two more and I could fix you for departure.
Polaris, as you say. And that's *our* star—
Northerly, northerly, all the seasons round.
I'll come for you at three, say, in the buggy
And we'll go out there. It's a marble stone,
Montpelier marble. Nothing but the name
And dates, you know. I couldn't find a text
That flattered Salem and did Canot justice.
At three then. You'll have sun to light you home
As suits a man who's listened the night out.
Before we die, we'll take that harbor cruise
Both of us, and after one last feel of sea
Let the ground have us, since the sea will not.

Chronology

April 15, 1918 Born at Manchester, New Hampshire; parents, Helen Eyre Osborne Coxe and Charles Shearman Coxe. 1940 Received B.A. from Princeton University. 1946 Married Edith Winsor; they have three sons, one daughter, and one grandson. 1947 *The Sea Faring and Other Poems* published by Henry Holt. 1948–1949 Briggs-Copeland Fellow, Harvard University. 1949–1955 Assistant-Associate Professor, University of Minnesota. 1953 With Robert Chapman, coauthored stage version of *Billy Budd*. 1955 *The Second Man and Other Poems* published by the University of Minnesota Press. 1955–present Pierce Professor of English, Bowdoin College, Brunswick, Maine. 1958 *The Wilderness and Other Poems* published by the University of Minnesota Press. 1959–1960 Fulbright professorship, Trinity College, Dublin. 1960 *The Middle Passage* published by the University of Chicago Press. 1962 Received Brandeis Award. 1962–1963 Visiting professor, at Princeton University. 1965 *The Last Hero and Other Poems* published by Vanderbilt University Press. 1966 *Nikal Seyn and Decoration Day: A Poem and a Play* published by Vanderbilt University Press. 1969 *Edwin Arlington Robinson: The Life of Poetry* published by Bobbs-Merrill. 1971–1972 Fulbright professorship, Universite de Provence, Aix-Marseille, France. 1976 *Enabling Acts: Selected Essays in Criticism* published by the University of Missouri Press, 1977 Received National Endowment for the Arts award. 1978 Awarded the Academy of American Poets Prize. Louis Coxe's poetry and essays have been published in numerous magazines, among them *The New Yorker, The New Republic, Poetry* (Chicago), *The Atlantic Monthly,* and *Sewanee Review.*

80049

PS
3505
09367
P55

COXE, LOUIS
PASSAGE.